THE FIRST SEASON:
1917–18 AND THE BIRTH OF THE NHL

THE FIRST SEASON:
1917–18 AND THE BIRTH OF THE NHL

BOB DUFF

BIBLIOASIS
WINDSOR, ONTARIO

FIRST EDITION

Library and Archives Canada Cataloguing in Publication

Duff, Bob, author
    The first season : 1917-18 and the birth of the NHL / Bob Duff.

Issued in print and electronic formats.
ISBN 978-1-77196-184-4 (softcover).--ISBN 978-1-77196-185-1 (ebook)

    1. National Hockey League--History. I. Title.

GV847.8.N3D836 2017   796.962'64   C2017-901961-9
                                                 C2017-901962-7

Edited by Daniel Wells
Copy-edited by Allana Amlin
Typeset by Chris Andrechek
Cover designed by Michel Vrana
Cover image: Eddie Livingstone's Toronto Blue Shirts, 1915.

Published with the generous assistance of the Canada Council for the Arts, which last year invested $153 million to bring the arts to Canadians throughout the country, and the financial support of the Government of Canada. Biblioasis also acknowledges the support of the Ontario Arts Council (OAC), an agency of the Government of Ontario, which last year funded 1,709 individual artists and 1,078 organizations in 204 communities across Ontario, for a total of $52.1 million, and the contribution of the Government of Ontario through the Ontario Book Publishing Tax Credit and the Ontario Media Development Corporation.

PRINTED AND BOUND IN CANADA

MIX
Paper from
responsible sources
FSC   FSC® C004071
www.fsc.org

CONTENTS

INTRODUCTION

One man built the National Hockey League. Or to be more precise, the distaste for one man laid the groundwork for the foundation of what would become the NHL.

If you were seeking to explain Eddie Livingstone to someone from the modern era, you would describe a man who was part Harold Ballard, part George Steinbrenner, with a smattering of P.T. Barnum mixed in for good measure.

The youngest of three children, Livingstone played juvenile and intermediate hockey for Toronto St. Georges. Later, he worked as a referee and as a sportswriter for the *Toronto Mail and Empire*. He sometimes was called upon to pen articles on the games he officiated.

When his playing and reffing days came to an end, Livingstone entered management. Working with a number of local amateur teams, Livvy, as he was known, exhibited the unique skills of a hockey bird dog, showing a keen eye for talent and team-building. He guided the Toronto Rugby and Athletic Association to back-to-back Ontario Hockey Association senior titles in 1913 and 1914.

Emboldened by this success, Livingstone decided to try his hand at the pro game. In 1914, he acquired ownership of the Toronto Ontarios, one of two National Hockey Association teams based in the Queen City. The NHA was the forerunner to the NHL, a major pro loop with teams based in Quebec and Ontario. Immediately, Livingstone set out to shake things up, switching the team's uniforms from a gaudy orange to Kelly green and renaming his club the Toronto Shamrocks.

Montreal Wanderers owner, Sam Lichtenhein.

Almost instantly, Livingstone began to butt heads with the NHA's old guard. He became the arch nemesis of Montreal Wanderers owner Sam Lichtenhein. During the 1914–15 season, the Shamrocks were forced to forfeit a game to the Wanderers because brothers Hal and George McNamara had gone home to be at the bedside of their gravely ill father and Livingstone couldn't ice enough players to proceed with the game.

After consideration, Lichtenhein offered to reschedule the game, but once he realized his team might need those two points to win the league title, Lichtenhein reneged on his promise and clung tightly to the two points gained from the forfeit. Livingstone demanded that Lichtenhein honour his word, and Lichtenhein countered by seeking to have Livingstone barred from the NHA.

The two men would feud constantly over the next few years. At a league meeting prior to the 1916–17 season, Lichtenhein offered Livingstone $3,000 for his team if he would promise to go away. Livingstone countered by dangling $5,000 in front of Lichtenhein for his team if the Montreal owner was willing to take a hike.

One year earlier, Frank Robinson, owner of the NHA's Toronto Blueshirts, enlisted in the Canadian armed forces, headed to the Great War and sold his team to Livingstone prior to his departure, giving Livingstone controlling interest in both Toronto clubs in the league. He was told to sell one of the teams, but when the rival

PCHA raided the Blueshirts and signed the majority of the roster, Livingstone traded his Shamrock players to the Blueshirts and folded the Shamrocks, leaving the NHA one team short.

Livingstone didn't seem to be happy unless he was fighting with someone. He battled over the cost of ice time at Toronto's Arena Gardens, threatening to pull his team out of the city and move it to Boston.

"Ever since he entered professional hockey, Eddie Livingstone has stirred things up, not only at the beginning of the season but all the way through it," the *Ottawa Journal* noted. "The Toronto magnate has been the regular old pepper-sauce of pro hockey since he broke into the game. And he was just as hot stuff when he had a team in the OHA and when he was also managing football clubs in the ORFU."

Shy of players due to the Great War, during the 1916–17 season the NHA enlisted a team comprised entirely of enlisted soldiers known as the 228th Battalion, who were also scheduled to play out of Toronto. But this plan went up in smoke mid-season when the 228th, also known as the Northern Fusiliers, received their orders to ship overseas and enter combat.

Left with an odd number of teams, the NHA owners decided the best solution was to cut both Toronto teams, and they suspended operations of Livingstone's Blueshirts.

Livvy was livid and filed a court injunction against the NHA to prevent the league's disposing of the Toronto franchise without his consent, but the move to remove Livingstone had its supporters, including the *Toronto Globe*. Without naming Livingstone, they wrote of his demise with gleeful delight, as one would welcome the breaking of a fever or the departure of unpleasant weather.

"The end of professional hockey in Toronto is not regretted by the well-wishers of sport," the *Globe* wrote in an editorial. "Whether that end is temporary or permanent depends on the temporary or permanent exclusion of the obnoxious element that is responsible for the present situation."

"From all accounts, the active clubs in the NHA do not mean to ever again permit the condition that offended the public to have any connection with the game in the future."

The owners of the other NHA clubs had heard enough from Livingstone. They wanted him gone. For good. While people could read about the exploits of the explorer Stanley and his search for Livingstone in the African jungle, the moguls who ran pro hockey in Canada would have happily paid someone to make their version of Livingstone disappear.

In the fall of 1917, they hatched a plan to make it happen. At the time, in the theatres, Canadian actress Mary Pickford was starring in The Little Princess. The book *Bringing Up Father* was the hot read, and for 30 cents a copy it would be yours.

A loaf of bread could be acquired for six cents and 24 pounds of flour would set you back $1.50. To heat your home, a cord of wood was valued at $2.50. If you wanted to emulate your hockey heroes, you'd ante up $2.50 for a decent pair of skates.

In the news, the front-page story was the tragic Halifax explosion that claimed nearly 2,000 lives. The sports section was dominated by tales of behemoth world heavyweight boxing champion Jess Willard. Known as the Pottawatomie Giant, Willard was a mountain of a man who stood 6–6 and tipped the scales at 235 pounds. But there was also plenty of talk about a young up and comer named Jack Dempsey, who many felt would soon step up to dethrone Willard.

In the midst of these goings-on, the NHL was born.

At Montreal's Windsor Hotel on October 20, 1917, the NHA owners gathered, minus Livingstone, and all of them resigned from the league in unison.

On November 26, 1917, they gathered again in the same hotel and formed a new league, again *sans* Livingstone, to be known as the National Hockey League. They might as well have told people that NHL stood for "Not Having Livingstone." Livingstone was left with no players, the NHL insisting that it owned all the Toronto contracts, and with 50 shares of a league in which he was the lone franchise.

It was only supposed to be a stop gap measure to rid themselves of the man they knew as the stormy petrel of hockey. The other owners figured Livingstone would skulk off into the sunset and they could reform the NHA without him in time for the 1918–19 season.

But they proved to be completely wrong. They underestimated Livvy's hatred for them, and his need for revenge, and for the next decade, he made it his personal mission to destroy the NHL.

Describing his ouster as a coup and a conspiracy, Livingstone was certain that when he had his day in court, and these backroom dealings were brought to light, it would show that everything had not been laid out according to Hoyle.

"He is known as one who would be willing perhaps to pay considerable out of his own pocket to cause any trouble possible for the NHL," the *Ottawa Journal* noted.

He fought the league in courtrooms for a decade, and ultimately won a small stipend, though he was never able to regain his team. But in the attempt, it's not a stretch to suggest that the bombastic Livingstone brought a much greater reward to the game of hockey, fortifying the rest of the owners in unison in opposition to him, and out of this unity a new league was born.

It's safe to say that were it not for Livingstone, the ongoing celebrations of a century of the NHL would not be taking place.

The Windsor Hotel, Montreal.

THE BIRTH OF PRO HOCKEY

It's difficult to determine which is more shocking: that the first professional hockey league began in, of all places, the tiny northern Michigan town of Houghton, or that it was begun by, of all people, a dentist.

John L. (Jack) Gibson was born and raised in the town of Berlin, Ontario, which, for obvious reasons, would be renamed Kitchener after the outbreak of the Great War. An outstanding hockey player, Gibson toiled for Berlin's top amateur club. Following a decisive 6–4 win over arch-rival Waterloo in 1898, each of Berlin's players was gifted a $10 gold coin by the mayor of Berlin. When word of this got back to the Ontario Hockey Association, all of Berlin's players were suspended. In the tight and restrictive code of the day as to what separated amateur from professional, even the rewarding of something as simple as a gift of gratitude was viewed as unacceptable in the eyes of those who governed sports.

Unable to play hockey in his home province, Gibson crossed the border to enroll at the Detroit College of Medicine, where he captained the hockey team while studying dentistry. The Detroit club played an exhibition game in Houghton and Gibson took a shine to the town. Upon graduation, he headed to Michigan's upper peninsula and set up a practice in Houghton in 1900.

The Berlin Hockey Club, 1897.

The local community soon came to know him as Doc Gibson, and the local hockey team came to know that not surprisingly, Gibson, a Canadian, was a pretty fair player. Merv Youngs, a new reporter at the local paper, the *Houghton Mining Gazette,* talked Gibson into joining the local team. He did so and before long, Gibson was named captain of the squad, known as the Portage Lakers.

Gibson began recruiting better players, first from among local talent, and later, by contacting friends and former teammates he knew in Canada. Gibson encouraged James Dee, a local businessman and a financial backer of the Lakers, to construct a new arena in Houghton, and the 2,500-seat Amphidrome opened in 1902. On December 29, 1902, the new rink was christened as the Portage club whipped the University of Toronto 13–2.

While this was going on in Michigan, there were also professional developments afoot in Pittsburgh. The construction of Duquesne Gardens, opened in 1896 as the first artificial ice rink in North America and with a capacity of 5,000, created the need for events to generate revenue for the vast ice house. Hockey helped to fill that bill.

As the steel capital of the United States, cash was plentiful in Pittsburgh and with so much disposable income available, the locals sought new entertainment experiences and hockey was an exciting option.

Those behind the money in the Steel City and who desired to export Canada's top winter sport south of the border were less up front about the payments that they were making to lure players to play hockey in Pennsylvania. "The demand upon Canadian players by the United States has reached such a pass that the hockey clubs themselves are thinking of taking some measures to put a stop to it," the *Montreal Star* reported. "Some clubs in the U.S. will pay almost anything to secure a winning team. Pittsburgh seems to be in the mecca of the hockey player."

Future Hockey Hall of Famers like goaltender Riley Hern and forward Alf Smith were lured to Pittsburgh. Though still officially listed as an amateur league, it was obvious to everyone in the game that Canada's top hockey players weren't heading to Pittsburgh for the scenery or culture. But the club found unique ways to hand paycheques to players.

"They make no bones whatever about paying men to play," an unnamed former Pittsburgh player told the *Montreal Star*. "I myself used to have a position of $15 per week. I had a room in a lawyer's office where I used to sit and write letters to myself." The faux job and weekly paycheque was merely a front, a cover-up to hide the task that these players were really being paid to perform. "Oh, I had a cinch," the anonymous player continued. "I was getting my $25 per week for playing hockey as regular as clockwork and with my arduous $15 a week job added to that, I did pretty well."

In Canada, the moguls who ran the game still looked upon professionalism with disdain. Even a hint of a player being offered any sort of remuneration for his services on the ice could lead to a player being banned from hockey for life. Those in charge of sports in Canada were of the opinion that professionalism was a taint on any game, that it brought the wrong element to sports and the wrong ideals, where winning was made a priority ahead of the simple thrill of athletic competition.

It must be remembered that the early sports organizations were the product of athletic clubs organized in the major Canadian cities by the upper crust of society and they viewed the purity of sport for the sake of sport. Playing sports was viewed as a recreational activity and not something to be pursued as a career choice.

Gibson set out to improve the talent pool for the 1903–04 season, and Portage became the first openly professional team in hockey. Among the recruits Gibson landed were three future Hockey Hall of Famers—centre Bruce Stuart, who led the club with 44 goals; Bruce's brother Hod, a defenceman who topped the team with 23 penalty minutes; and goaltender Riley Hern, lured from Pittsburgh, posted a sterling 13–1 record with a 1.50 goals-against average and four shutouts.

Portage was the best team of a four-team league in the Michigan U.P., a loop that also included the towns of Hancock, Laurium and Sault Ste. Marie, Michigan. Including exhibition matches, Portage won 24 of 26 games that season and even defeated the Montreal Wanderers, one of the top amateur teams in Canada, in a two-game series in late March of 1904, winning by 8–4 and 9–2 counts.

The series, played March 21–22, 1904, was touted as the world's championship of hockey in the local paper, the *Daily Mining Gazette*. "The Wanderers of Montreal have challenged the Portage Lakes for the championship of the world," the paper reported on March 18, 1904. "C.E. Webb, manager of the Portage Lake hockey team, received a communication last night from the manager of the Wanderers of Montreal in which he challenged the Portage Lakes for the championship of the world. The Wanderers are considered to be one of the fastest teams in existence and are anxious to meet the Portage Lake aggregation at any time or place.

"The expense of bringing the Montreal team here will be very great, but it is thought that this difficulty will be overcome. Mr.

Webb will communicate with the Wanderers' management at once and will endeavor to make satisfactory arrangement for a series of games and there is little doubt that the residents for Portage Lake will be able to witness a game for the championship of the world at the Amphidrome some time during the coming week."

Art Ross.

The Wanderers then travelled to Pittsburgh and were defeated in two of three meetings with the local Victorias club.

Previously on March 2, 1904, the same Wanderers, whose roster included future Hockey Hall of Famers Art Ross and Jimmy Gardner, had faced the Stanley Cup champion Ottawa Hockey Club—the famous Silver Seven, as they were known—in the Federal Hockey League final and battled them to a 5–5 draw in a challenge game for the Cup. Billed as the dirtiest game that two senior teams had ever played, 36 penalties were assessed and it was a contest that left a sour taste in the mouths of some spectators, among them R.J. Whitelaw, president of the Winnipeg Victorias hockey club, Stanley Cup champions in 1900–01 and 1901–02.

So violent was the game that the Wanderers declined to travel to Ottawa to complete the series.

"The spirit of professionalism has crept into the game and there was evinced a win or die determination, which resulted in a game utterly unworthy of the best spirit of honest amateurism," Whitelaw told the *Montreal Gazette*. "In comparison with former games played for the Stanley Cup, I must say that if this was representative of present day hockey, then the game has deteriorated and degenerated into a struggle where strength and roughness are great factors in determining superiority.

"In the former matches, the players went on the ice to test their skill, and were satisfied that when defeated, the better team had won."

Whitelaw's assessment, in a nutshell, emphasized the disdainful view those in positions of power within the game in Canada held toward what they viewed as the scourge of professionalism. Even the slightest hint of pro activity, of accepting any sort of remuneration of gift in return for playing any game, was dealt with swiftly and harshly, generally with lifetime bans from all sport. It was a disciplinary measure originally spearheaded by the Ontario Hockey Association, but later adopted by both the Canadian Amateur Hockey Association and the Amateur Athletic Union of Canada.

The people in charge of these organizations were men of money, power and influence, and they swung the weight of their influence with forceful authority. The champion of this train of thought was OHA president John Ross Robertson. A powerful man—the Ontario Hockey League's championship trophy still bears his name—Robertson was a Member of Parliament and publisher of the Toronto Telegram, which he utilized as a bully pulpit to campaign against what he viewed as the blight of professionalism. Those accused of professionalism were considered to be guilty first and required to offer proof of their innocence before they would be allowed to resume playing.

Robertson viewed any man who would pursue sport for profit, as opposed to the simple love of the game, to be not only disrespectful of polite society, but also disloyal to the country. Quietly, the powers that be behind amateur sport also viewed the value of athletic competition to be a way of maintaining fit young men who could quickly be organized into a military force in times of armed conflict.

Regardless, the movement of many of the best Canadian amateurs to industrial centres in northern Michigan and Pittsburgh, where the U.S. economy was booming and arena facilities were already in place, set off alarm bells in the birthplace of hockey. As much as Canadian hockey leaders disdained professionalism, it was evident from the results of the Wanderers matches in Houghton and Pittsburgh that if something wasn't done to reverse the drain on the talent pool, Canadian hockey and thus the competition for the Stanley Cup, would become a second-tier event.

At this juncture in hockey history, it appeared the only silver of interest to the world's best players wasn't the silver of Lord Stanley's mug, but that which could line their pockets by heading south.

Some top players even questioned the value of the Stanley Cup competition. "The Cup is far from beneficial to the game, it is a detriment to it," Montreal Amateur Athletic Association captain Dickie Boon suggested to the *Montreal Star* in 1903. Boon felt the competition for the Cup was growing more cut-throat and that there were backroom deals quietly afoot to lure top players to switch teams.

Gibson and Dee seized on this unrest in Canada to drive a new idea to the fore—an entirely professional league. Financial backing for such a venture would not be an issue. The mining boom in northern Michigan, in what became known as Copper Country, turned the area into the place for both the wealthy and for those in search of wealth. And many of those folks were transplanted Canadians like Gibson, single men with plenty of money and little in the way of expenses, and they wanted their hockey and were willing to pay handsomely to see it.

Today a town with a population of 35,000, during the mining boom Houghton's population exploded from 9,000 to 100,000. Ten trains a day connected the tiny town to major centres such as Chicago, Detroit, Milwaukee and Minneapolis. At the time, over 70 percent of the copper used in the United States was produced in this part of the country.

Gibson designed a comprehensive plan for his pro league. There would be a revenue sharing program to ensure the financial stability of all clubs. An ambitious 24-game schedule was drawn up. Originally slated to be called the American Hockey Association, teams would be located in Houghton (to be known as Portage Lake), Pittsburgh, Calumet and Sault Ste. Marie, Michigan. But when Sault Ste. Marie, Ontario also exhibited interest in a club, that city was accepted and the league was christened with a new name—the International Hockey League.

Becoming the first pro hockey team in Canadian history wasn't what drove the people behind the franchise in Sault Ste. Marie, Ontario. Their reasons were much more personal. "The town wanted a team that could lick the American Soo," Canadian Soo Arena Company president J.C. Boyd told the *Sault Ste. Marie Evening News*.

League play opened December 4, 1904, at Duquesne Gardens, where Portage Lake doubled Pittsburgh 6–3 and Barney Holden netted the first goal in IHL history.

The rosters were dotted with a who's who of that hockey era. Besides Gibson, Portage also suited up Bruce Stuart, Riley Hern, and Charlie Liffiton, a Stanley Cup winner with the Montreal AAA in 1901–02. Hod Stuart, Jimmy Gardner, Ken Mallen, and goalie Billy Nicholson played for Calumet. Pittsburgh signed Tom Melville, later an NHL referee, and the Sixsmith brothers, Art and Garnet. The Canadian Soo listed future Hall of Famer Oliver Seibert, while the Canadian Soo roster included two original NHLers—forwards Didier Pitre and Jack Laviolette, both of whom would play for the Montreal Canadiens in 1917–18.

Didier Pitre.

Jack Laviolette.

So popular was the league that local saloons began installing telephones simply to be able to call opposing rinks when the home team was on the road, so those gathered at their favourite watering hole could obtain instant updates from the games. Extra trains were added on game days to transport fans from one city to another within the league.

As word spread of the money to be made playing hockey in the IHL, top players scrambled to cash in. The legendary Fred (Cyclone) Taylor, the Wayne Gretzky of this era, joined the Portage Lakers in 1905–06, along with Joe Hall, who would play defence for the Canadiens in the NHL's inaugural season of 1917–18.

The passion for hockey in these towns was apparent. "[Houghton was] a great Saturday night fun place for miners who prefer to patronize something other than art museums or the opera house," Taylor expressed.

Newsy Lalonde, an original NHLer with the Canadiens and a two-time NHL scoring champion, signed with the Canadian Soo, as did the McNamara brothers, George and Hal and goalie Hugh Lehman. All would earn Stanley Cup inscriptions during their careers. Ernie Liffiton and Tommy Smith, the latter a future NHLer, joined Pittsburgh.

Calumet won the IHL title in 1904–05 and Portage Lake were champions in 1905–06 and 1906–07. After each of their titles, the team from Houghton issued a challenge for Lord Stanley's mug to the trustees of the Stanley Cup, but it fell on deaf ears, with the trustees of the Cup having no interest in getting involved in the professional-amateur debate.

Meanwhile, a mining boom was also exploding in Northern Ontario and several top stars headed there to play in the newly formed Temiskaming Mine League. Often, players from the IHL would slip into these towns such as Haileybury and Cobalt, suiting up as ringers, playing under assumed names. It was nothing more than clandestine professionalism. Teams from this league also challenged for the Stanley Cup and were rejected because they were more shamateur than amateur.

Behind the scenes, Canadian hockey officials were very aware of the impact of the IHL. They understood that it threatened the very existence of major-league hockey in the place where the game originated. Amateur hockey's bosses tried to remain staunchly resistant to professionalizing their sport. OHA president John Ross Robertson, a man often referred to as the father of amateur hockey, continued to be the most ardent critic of the pro game and fought tooth and nail to prevent its advent in Canada.

"Sports should be pursued for its own sake," Robertson noted in an address to the OHA. Robertson maintained his assault on professionalism as publisher of the *Toronto Telegram,* launching a steady campaign of anti-professional propaganda in the pages of his broadsheet. "Any players who figure on these [pro] leagues must be banished from Ontario hockey."

He felt that the advent of professionalism was a stain on the great game of hockey and would lead to excess violence on the ice by creating a win-at-all-costs attitude rather than the pursuit of sport that the pureness of amateurism created. He viewed pros as nothing more than ruffians.

This hard and firm approach was beginning to bend in other Canadian centres, however. At the time, Toronto had never won a Stanley Cup. Teams from Montreal and Ottawa dominated the competition for Lord Stanley's mug and the handlers of the teams in these cities feared that their sport could become irrelevant if top talent continued to leave the league for the opportunity to play for more money elsewhere.

Already, lacrosse had loosened its rules and permitted pros to play alongside amateurs in 1905, and there was growing support for this type of scenario in some hockey centres in Eastern Canada.

"I believe the boys will find the ground all ready for the seed of professional hockey," J.E. McNamara, manager of the Portage Lakers IHL team, told the *Winnipeg Tribune* in March of 1906. "It has been the national winter game of Canada for many years.

There is no doubt that they could work a professional league to great advantage."

Not everyone shared McNamara's optimism. "As far as I am personally concerned, you can say that I will have nothing to do with having a professional hockey [club] at the Auditorium rink next season," Albert E. Fulljames, manager of the Winnipeg rink, told the *Winnipeg Tribune* at the same time of McNamara's statement.

Meanwhile, it was revealed that there was no reason that the Cup had to go to an amateur team. "There is a mistaken impression current that the Stanley Cup is a trophy for amateur teams pure and simple," the *Ottawa Journal* noted. "The trophy is simply supposed to represent the hockey championship of Canada, and nothing is mentioned in the deed of gift as to the clubs being amateur."

By fall 1906, there was strong speculation of a pro hockey league emerging in Montreal. "There is some startling hockey news referring to the probable reorganization of the existing hockey union," the *Montreal Star* noted.

It was reported that the Montreal AAA, Shamrocks, Nationals, Victorias and the Quebec Hockey Club, were all set to leave the Canadian Amateur Hockey League and join the Montreal Wanderers and Ottawa Hockey Club—commonly referred to as the Silver Seven—of the Federal League in a new loop. But that wasn't even the biggest news.

"The reorganization of the hockey union will be brought about by the introduction of professionalism," the *Montreal Star* reported. There was also speculation about another pro loop forming in western Ontario involving Brantford, Guelph, Berlin, Toronto and perhaps even Stratford or Woodstock.

Jimmy Gardner, who was back in town from his duties with the IHL team in Calumet, was a strong proponent of this idea and threatened to leak information to the press and league about some of the so-called amateurs who were being paid handsomely under the table to stay with their Canadian clubs.

At an October 27, 1906, meeting of the Canadian Amateur Athletic Union in Montreal, it was ruled that teams could either turn pro or stay amateur, but that the two types of players could not share the same ice without jeopardizing the amateur's standing. Frank Grierson of Ottawa, vice-president of the CAAU, stated that he knew of three hockey players who'd made over $1,350 the previous season and if they did not come forward as pros, he would publicly out them. A committee was established by the CAAU to investigate Grierson's charges.

This debate about the relationship between amateur and professional players raged for most of the month. The Montreal AAA announced in early November that it would withdraw from the CAAU unless the organization would support a proposal that would allow pros and amateurs to play side by side.

On November 10, 1906, the issue was finally settled. A new group—the Eastern Canada Amateur Hockey Association—was formed at a meeting at the Windsor Hotel in Montreal, the same building in which the NHL would be born 11 years later. The new organization was built on the principle of allowing amateurs and pros to play side by side in competition without impacting the status of the amateur player. The six teams immediately tendered their resignations from the CAAU. Fred McRobie was named president of the ECAHA.

The only condition was that every club in the league would be required to publish a list of which of its players were pros and which had opted to maintain their amateur standing. The lists would be printed in the newspaper so that there would be no question as to who was who in hockey.

In Ontario, OHA head Robertson was apoplectic over this decision. "You know, Abe Lincoln said the Union could not exist half slave and half free. I believe that the OHA cannot honourably be half amateur and half professional."

Regardless of what he thought about it, there was no way to turn back now. The pro game was exploding across Canada. Another new professional league was founded at the same time, with teams in Brandon, Winnipeg, Portage la Prairie and Kenora, Ontario.

It didn't take long for the pros who had left Canada for more lucrative contracts in the United States to begin to find their way home. The Montreal Wanderers signed goalie Riley Hern, an IHL veteran, who had most recently played for the IHL Portage Lakers, on November 18, 1906, only eight days after the formation of the ECAHA.

This allowance, however, of teams to have both professional and amateur players created other problems. Teams were quickly hit by requests for more money from players who understood that this might be an opportunity to cash in. Frank (Pud) Glass jumped from the Montreal AAA to the Wanderers for a salary of $750 and Gordon Davidson also left the AAA's and signed with the Montreal Victorias, to take just two examples. Whoever could pay the most money could quickly assemble the most talented roster.

The Montreal AAA club, known as the Winged Wheelers and first winners of the Stanley Cup back in 1892–93, fought back, insisting those players were under contract to play with their club.

"I don't know whether or not he signed any other contract," Wanderers secretary W. Jennings told the *Montreal Gazette*. "I know we have this one."

Russell Bowie of the Victorias was astonished that anyone would question Davidson's decision to join their club. "Well you know Davidson just had to play with the Vics," Bowie explained. "Why he couldn't play anywhere else. All his chums are in the club."

Meanwhile, in Ottawa, two of the stars of the famed Stanley Cup champion Silver Seven—Frank McGee and Harvey Pulford—were taking advantage of these changes to hold out for better contracts.

History was made on December 27, 1906, as the Wanderers blasted New Glasgow, Nova Scotia, 10–3 in the opener of their two-game Stanley Cup series. Goalie Riley Hern, who had played in the IHL before the ECAHA was formed, centre Frank (Pud)

Glass and right winger Ernie (Moose) Johnson all saw action for the Wanderers, becoming the first pros to ever play in a Stanley Cup game.

Pro hockey in Canada was here to stay.

The Canadian Hockey League, consisting of Toronto, Berlin, Brantford and Galt, began play in 1907–08, which meant that Canada now had three pro leagues. The loss, however, of all of the top Canadian talent meant that the IHL died a quiet death back in U.S. copper country following the 1906–07 season, no longer able to lure players south of the border now that the playing field was levelled.

Though the formation of the ECAHA and the other professional leagues in Canada marked the beginning of the professionalization of hockey, that didn't mean that these initial leagues were put together in a thorough, planned and professional manner. Many of the things that we would take for granted today with professional sports were not put in place in the earliest professional leagues. Contracts, for instance, were poorly thought out and full of loopholes which created as many problems as they solved. There were no clauses of any sort in early pro-hockey contracts tying a player to a particular team, so contract jumping was frequent, especially during Stanley Cup competition, when players became mercenaries available to the highest bidder. Nor was any sort of salary structure put in place.

Pittsburgh was paying Hod Stuart $1,250 for a 12-game season in 1906–07 at a time when the average annual salary in the United States was $523. Ottawa paid Tom Phillips $1,600 for the 1907–08 season. When the Edmonton Pros challenged for the Stanley Cup in 1908–09, they proved to be the most mercenary of clubs. For that series alone, Phillips, Didier Pitre, Lester Patrick, Steve Vair and Hal McNamara were recruited as paid ringers. This early tumult made those who opposed the professionalization of hockey seem prescient, as the leagues almost immediately develop a mercenary aspect.

By 1907, there was strong speculation that the formation of a major international pro league was on the horizon, with American cities such as Detroit, Cleveland, New York, Boston, Chicago, Pittsburgh and Columbus seen as potential locations. It wouldn't unfold as quickly as anticipated, but eventually all of these major American centres would house NHL franchises.

In 1909, infighting among team owners, a trend that would become commonplace in the first decade of professional hockey, brought about the demise of the ECHA (the word amateur was ultimately dropped from the league's handle). The league was disbanded on November 25, 1909, and the Ottawa Senators and Montreal Shamrocks continued on to form the nucleus of a new league, the six-team Canadian Hockey Association.

Meanwhile, sparked by the mining boom happening concurrently in Northern Ontario and backed by the wealth of Renfrew, Ontario, dairy magnate J. Ambrose O'Brien, a rival league was born, the National Hockey Association, including former ECHA members of the Montreal Wanderers and teams in Renfrew, as well as the mining towns of Haileybury and Cobalt, Ontario. O'Brien also supported the suggestion of Wanderers' manager Jimmy Gardner to assemble a fifth team for the league, a club comprised of French-speaking players that would be called the Montreal Canadiens, and provided Jack Laviolette the financial backing to do so.

Once again, the new league was formed during a meeting at Montreal's Windsor Hotel—another trend that would continue in Canadian pro hockey.

As soon as the new league was formed, teams began to battle for players, with larger salaries and purses paid than ever before in professional hockey history. The first owner to literally try to buy a Stanley Cup champion, J. Ambrose O'Brien paid Lester Patrick $3,000 and his brother Frank $2,000 to play in Renfrew, and anted up a whopping $5,250 to get Cyclone Taylor's name on a contract, making Taylor the second-highest paid athlete in North America. Only Detroit Tigers outfielder Ty Cobb,

The Renfrew Creamery Kings.

at $6,500, earned a higher stipend than Taylor. But Cobb was required to work 154 games to garner his paycheque. Taylor only suited up for a dozen.

O'Brien even offered Hay Miller, who was in the east to play for Edmonton in an upcoming Stanley Cup series, $1,000 to play one game for Renfrew. Amazingly, Miller declined the payday. Technically, the Renfrew club was known as the Creamery Kings, but everyone simply branded them the Millionaires.

Other teams were forced to compete for top players, placing tremendous pressure on their already threatened bottom lines. The result of this financial insanity was quick and decisive: on January 15, 1910, the CHA disbanded. The Senators and Shamrocks were absorbed into the NHA fold.

With just one pro league in operation, it was time to reign in the cost of professionalism. When the 1910–11 season arrived, the landscape of the NHA had changed dramatically. Small-town Haileybury and Cobalt were gone, as were the Shamrocks. In came the Quebec Bulldogs and a new owner for the Canadiens, former professional wrestler and wrestling promoter George Kennedy. Kennedy claimed ownership of a trademark of the name Club Athletique Canadien and threatened to sue, so was sold the club for $7,500, about $2,500 more than O'Brien originally put up to outfit the team.

At the NHA's annual meeting on November 12, 1910—at the Windsor Hotel, of course—T. Emmett Quinn was named league president and a hard salary cap of $5,000 per team was introduced to provide the league with cost certainty.

"With the club salary limit of $5,000 adopted, the next business will be whipping the players into line," the *Montreal Gazette* suggested. "There will, without a doubt, be a strenuous kick all along the line at the salary reductions from the ridiculous figures of last season, but if the league sits tight it can control the situation."

The *Gazette* proclaimed a grave future for the game if the salary governor did not take effect.

"If it does not control it this winter, then it is a case of goodbye to professional hockey," the *Gazette* predicted.

There was also another interesting development from the meeting: "There was some discussion among the delegates as to giving the Canadian Athletic Club the option on all French-Canadian players, but no decision was reached," the *Gazette* reported. It was felt that by creating a team with a strong French-Canadian flavour in the league, it would help draw more French-speaking Montrealers to watch pro hockey.

As anticipated, it was the salary cap that became front-page news. "Why I would rather quit the game than accept the sum which is allotted to me according to the NHA rules," Ottawa Senators left winger Dubbie Kerr complained to the *Ottawa Journal*. "Just imagine a player taking the bumps the National stars do, with the chance of getting maimed for life, and then expect a man to go out and play up to his standard for about half, or perhaps less, than the amount he was given last season for exactly the same work."

Others begged to differ. Ottawa player Ted Dey, a Stanley Cup winner in 1909, called the salary cap, "the salvation of hockey.

"Hockey would not last another winter at the prices the promoters were forced to pay last winter, and I foresaw, even then, that the prices must take a tumble," Dey told the *Journal*.

There was little choice in the matter. With only one major pro league in operation in the country, they could either take the lowered pay or take a hike.

What was a fellow to do?

The Patricks had a few thoughts in that regard, and soon would share them with the hockey world.

On December 7, 1911, Frank and Lester Patrick, bankrolled by the millions their father Joe made in the lumber business in British Columbia, announced the formation of the Pacific Coast Hockey Association.

Once again, the players had options and were in the driver's seat, and it wasn't long before the cry of "Go west, young man," was being heeded by the world's top puck-chasing talent.

Skinner Poulin, Walter Smaill and Bobby Rowe headed to the coast to join Lester Patrick's club in Victoria, B.C. Renfrew's Bert Lindsay, the father of Hall of Famer Ted Lindsay and the fellow who would eventually get the win in the NHL's first game, was in goal.

Vancouver, Frank Patrick's squad, was also a who's who of hockey talent—Tom Phillips and Si Griffis from Kenora's Stanley Cup winning team of 1906–07 and Renfrew's Newsy Lalonde, also destined to be a first-year NHLer.

New Westminster, the third club, included Ernie Johnson, Harry Hyland and Jimmy Gardner from the Wanderers and goalie Hugh Lehman from the Ontario Pro League.

The PCHA was operating on a level not seen before in the Canadian pro game. While the eastern squads were all associated with traditional sporting clubs, some of which still included amateur players, these were stand-alone, all-professional hockey-only teams. And the Patrick family owned each of the teams. Players did not sign a contract with their team, they inked a personal services pact with the Patrick family.

The raiding of players from the east only ramped up the next season, the PCHA's prize possession coming when Vancouver lured Cyclone Taylor to the coast. At the end of

The 1912–13 Stanley Cup winning Quebec Bulldogs.

the 1912–13 season, the PCHA champion Victoria Aristocrats issued a Stanley Cup challenge to title holders, the NHA's Quebec Bulldogs. The challenge was denied, but Quebec headed west for an exhibition series regardless, and promptly lost two of three games.

The following spring, the PCHA champion Victoria club went east to face the Stanley Cup champion Toronto Blueshirts and opted to cut out the middleman, not even bothering to issue a formal challenge for the Cup, as was required in the day. It didn't matter. Toronto swept all three games.

The first official East-West Stanley Cup series was held in 1914–15 and it was no contest. The NHA champion Senators travelled from Ottawa to Vancouver and were whipped in three straight by the Millionaires by a combined score of 26–8.

The 1915–16 Cup final was also a momentous occasion, as the Canadiens downed the PCHA champion Portland Rosebuds. It was the first of 24 Stanley Cup wins for the Habs and the Oregon city became the first American club to compete for Lord Stanley's mug. The Seattle Metropolitans took it one step further in the spring of 1917, defeating the Canadiens to become the first American team to win the Cup.

The 1917 Seattle Metropolitans, the first American team
to win the Stanley Cup.

Just when it appeared that pro hockey was finally on stable
footing, world politics pulled the rug out from under the professional sports ranks. The outbreak of the Great War in Europe
sent many young Canadian men off to fight, including several
top hockey players such as Frank McGee and Scotty Davidson,
and left people back home to question the value and importance
of hockey games.

Recognizing the distinct possibility that hockey could
be declared a non-essential industry to the war effort, NHA
owners sought to make a patriotic display. For the 1916–17
season, they included an all-military franchise, the 228th
Battalion, comprised of hockey players who had enlisted in
the Canadian Forces, featuring star players such as Gordon
(Duke) Keats, Hal McNamara, Art Duncan and Goldie
Prodger, although Toronto owner Eddie Livingstone was
openly critical of the team, insisting that some of the players
weren't in the military at all.

There were benefits to this move. It was claimed that all the
team's profits were going directly to the war effort. And with

so many hockey players enlisting, the team gave the shrinking NHA another franchise to fill out the schedule.

Or at least it did so for a time. Amidst some negative publicity about soldiers playing pro hockey while others were dying in the trenches of France, on February 8, 1917, the NHA was left shy a team when the 228th Battalion was ordered overseas, leaving the league with five teams.

Three days later, the NHA owners convened a meeting—yes, at the Windsor Hotel—and suggested that in order to leave an even-numbered group in the league, voted to suspend the Toronto franchise for the remainder of the season. In reality, they saw it as a way to rid themselves, at least temporarily, of bombastic Toronto owner Eddie Livingstone.

Conveniently, Livingstone was absent from the gathering. "I had a very painful boil on the back of my neck," Livingstone explained.

The other NHA owners considered Livingstone to be a very painful boil on their own necks, and seemed happy to have it lanced.

They had originally welcomed Livingstone with open arms when he put an NHA club in Toronto in 1912, one of two to join the league in the Queen City that season. But while the Blueshirts flourished, Toronto's other club—owned by Livingstone and known as the Tecumsehs, then the Ontarios, and finally the Shamrocks—were regular basement dwellers. Livingstone feuded with the managers of Toronto's Mutual Street Arena and at one point, threatened to relocate his team to Boston.

In 1915, Blueshirts owner Frank Robinson enlisted in the army and his team was sold, purchased by none other than Livingstone, who now owned both Toronto franchises.

He was ordered by the league to sell one of the teams. Instead, Livingstone went against their wishes and folded the Shamrocks, moving the Shamrocks players to the Blueshirts, and leaving the league with an odd number of franchises at five, making scheduling a more difficult process.

By 1916, the other NHA owners had had their fill of Livingstone and his antics. "The belief exists locally that Toronto may never be taken back," the *Ottawa Citizen* reported. "The Queen City has been a thorn in the side of the NHA ever since their franchises were granted.

"This season ought to have been a hummer in Toronto, but Eddie Livingstone and [the 228th Battalion] declared war on one another before the season and their inability to deal with their problems in a sportsmanlike way led to so much scragging that the welfare of the league there has been seriously impaired.

"Livingstone has antagonized hundreds at Toronto and the club itself became decidedly unpopular."

The story was half right. The owners weren't done with Toronto. But they'd had more than enough of Livingstone, and would come up with a novel way to deal with the problem.

The Toronto 228th Battalion, 1917.

THE NHL IS BORN

The hockey that was taking place in Canada's pro game during the winter of 1917 was hardly recognizable to long-time fans. Most of the top pro players had already departed, exchanging their sticks and skates for rifles and boots, signing up with the Canadian Armed Forces to join the fight on the other side of the Atlantic Ocean in the Great War, leaving the old, infirm and unqualified to carry on between the boards.

After the 228th Battalion team left the NHA mid-season to go to the front lines during the 1916–17 season, there simply wasn't enough talented professional-level players to fill the top-flight hockey league the NHA had become.

Clearly, something had to change.

The NHA executive met on October 20, 1917, at Montreal's Windsor Hotel to discuss the future of their league. Rumours were rampant. Ottawa Senators forward Jack Darragh predicted that the NHA, a six-team league at the commencement of the 1916–17 season, would be reduced to a three-team outfit.

The news from the meeting was that the moguls planned to hold firm with the four teams that had wrapped up the 1916–17 NHA—the champion Montreal Canadiens, the Montreal Wanderers, the Ottawa Hockey Club and the Quebec Bulldogs. Toronto, which had been dropped from the loop when the

228th Battalion squad was shipped overseas it was agreed, would not be readmitted to the league.

The justifications provided by the league's owners were centred on the war overseas and its effects on the game. With so many of the league's star players in the trenches of Europe, there simply weren't enough quality skaters to fill five or six teams. Besides, the owners reasoned, a larger league would require more scheduled games, and this might prove selfish: at a time when everyone had to do without, sacrificing and rationing in support of the war effort, a longer hockey season would be unpatriotic. What the owners tried to keep from the public, however, was the fact that a completely different war was still being fought in the NHA's boardroom, the purpose of which was to remove Toronto owner Eddie Livingstone and the many problems he brought with him. "There was renewed determination on the part of the Ottawa, Montreal and Quebec clubs not to tolerate the Toronto owner any longer," reported the *Toronto Globe*.

"Should Mr. Livingstone try by means of injunction or otherwise to interfere with the eastern schedule as proposed, it looks as if the only thing for the National Hockey Association to do would be to commit Hari Kari or immolate itself upon a funeral pyre, from the ashes of which, like the fabled Phoenix, a new senior professional hockey body would arise," the *Montreal Star* predicted.

This was indeed the novel idea the NHA franchise owners had come up with to solve their Livingstone dilemma behind the Windsor Hotel's closed doors.

"National Hockey Association suspends operation for year," the *Ottawa Citizen* announced. "New league will replace it. Five clubs wished to play but only four will do so. Ottawa sure of franchise. Eastern League will likely be launched this week and if Quebec drops out Toronto Arena Company will place a sextet in it."

Technically, the news report wasn't accurate. The NHA hadn't been shut down at all.

As the meeting adjourned, reporter Elmer Ferguson of the *Montreal Herald* retired with the Montreal owners to the hotel bar to get the scoop.

"Don't get us wrong," Wanderers owner Sam Lichtenhein explained to Ferguson. "We didn't throw Livingstone out. He's still got his franchise in the old National Hockey Association.

"We didn't throw Eddie Livingstone out. Perish the thought. That would have been illegal and unfair. Also, it wouldn't have been sporting.

"He has his team, and we wish him well. The only problem is he's playing in a one-team league."

Ferguson originally referred to this new loop as the Livingstoneless League.

"The present situation has taught a lesson to the NHA," Montreal Canadiens owner/manager George Kennedy said, "If a new league is organized, as I expect it will be, there will no doubt be provision made for getting rid of any undesirable member, through the unanimous vote of all the directors.

"The only way in which we can expel a member now is by getting out ourselves."

The bonds each owner had signed, which had guaranteed each NHA club would continue as members of the league, had expired on October 1, so there was nothing to prevent the clubs from suspending operations and forming a new league.

Word soon spread about how the NHA owners had frozen out the black ace of their group.

"Livvy can have the NHA all to himself to do what he likes with it," the *Ottawa Journal* reported on October 24, 1917. "The Ottawa, Wanderer, Canadien and Quebec clubs will resign from that organization and form a new league."

There was speculation that this new league would be called Eastern Canada Hockey League, but the Eastern Canada Amateur Hockey Association protested, fearing it would lead to confusion. The Union Hockey Association was also proposed. There was also a suggestion put forth at the meeting to place all

Ken Randall.

five team names into hat and draw the one that would be inoperative.

"While I have nothing to say, I cannot presume to imagine what the incoming executive of the National AAA may do," Ottawa club president A.L. Caron told the *Montreal Star*.

There was rampant talk in Toronto that the owners of the other NHA franchises, who'd usurped Livingstone's players when the Toronto team was forced to suspend operations during the 1916–17 campaign, weren't anxious to part with their new-found chattel.

"There is a well-founded suspicion that one reason why the eastern members of the National Hockey Association are eager to crowd the Toronto club out of the pro hockey combine is because they are short of players," the *Toronto Daily News* claimed. "It would be a fine thing for the Wanderers if they could corral [Ken] Randall, [Harry] Cameron and [Alf] Skinner. The Canadiens could also use Reg Noble to advantage while the Ottawa club could find a place for Corbett Denneny without much trouble. Quebec needed a goalkeeper and Sammy Hebert would prove a fitting substitute for the decrepit Paddy Moran. These eastern hockey moguls are a foxy lot of individuals. They do not overlook many tricks.

"For the past two years they have made every effort to freeze out Livingstone's club but 'Very Good Eddie' has been too much for them. He beat them in the courts and in the committee room and will likely down them again."

The fact that all of this petty infighting was happening at a time when many young men, including some of professional hockey's leading stars, were making the ultimate sacrifice and risking their lives during the Great War wasn't doing pro hockey any favours in the court of public opinion.

"The pro hockey clubs will install themselves into public disfavor pretty soon if they don't look out," the *Ottawa Journal* warned.

It was also obvious that Livingstone, whatever the claims of the other hockey moguls, was not the only problem facing major league hockey. For starters, Quebec didn't appear to be on a solid footing at all. The Bulldogs were hurting for players. To add insult to injury, Quebec City's top senior amateur team, the Sons of Ireland, often drew larger crowds than the Bulldogs, something which also happened in Toronto and other cities with pro franchises.

In order to improve the team both on the ice and in the accountant's ledger entries, the Bulldogs tried to convince some of the Sons of Ireland players to turn pro, though this proved unsuccessful. As the deadline for forming a new league, setting down a schedule and booking arena dates drew closer, there was no resolution apparent from the Ancient Capital club, as Quebec City's team was also known.

"It would appear as if the time has arrived when the Quebec Hockey Club must announce what it intends to do this winter," the *Ottawa Journal* noted on November 17, 1917. "Every day during the past week, a different story has come out of the Ancient Capital regarding the intentions of the Bulldogs. One day they are going to operate a team in the new Eastern Canada Hockey Association; the next day they have decided to suspend for the winter.

"A show down at once is imperative. Or, rather the Ottawa, Wanderer and Canadien clubs should meet at once and take Toronto late into the circuit. Both Eddie Livingstone and the Toronto Arena Company are ready to operate this season if given the opportunity. They can go ahead at once, when the Quebec club keeps dilly dallying. It appears useless for the other clubs to wait on the far eastern club any longer."

The reasons for Quebec's indecisiveness were well-known to all in and around the game. And most of them came down to insufficient funding.

"It is a fact known to everyone that the financial condition of the Quebec Hockey Club has been darker than ever these last two seasons and with the present prospects there seems to be no way out of the trouble," the *Ottawa Journal* reported.

"Thursday night, [Quebec manager] Mike Quinn wired the Ottawa, Canadien and Wanderer clubs inquiring if they desired to buy some of the Quebec players."

Quebec's future was not the only problem facing the incipient league. If the other owners had presumed that Livingstone would go away quietly, they were sadly mistaken.

After originally suggesting that he was done with pro hockey, Livingstone vowed to pay his players a salary not to play or to participate in a series of barnstorming exhibition games rather than let them go to other teams.

That idea didn't sit well with the Toronto players. "Livingstone didn't pay me in 1916 and 1917," Toronto captain Ken Randall said. "How can a contract still hold me?"

Livingstone, who was supposed to hand over control of his team to lawyer John F. Boland or Charles Querrie, manager of Toronto's Mutual Street Arena, took out an injunction against the Ottawa club, the first of many court proceedings he would initiate.

There was speculation that Livingstone's Toronto players might go on waivers, be divided up among the other clubs and that some would jump to the rival PCHA on the West Coast.

Lichtenhein, Livingstone's most ardent enemy, denied that Livingstone had been aced out of their league. "The Toronto club seems to labour under the impression that it has been 'frozen out,'" Lichtenhein said. "I was told that the club will insist on playing."

Meanwhile, behind the scenes, both Lichtenhein and Kennedy sought a four-team league or no league at all.

"As for the Wanderers, I can say that this club will positively not participate in any five-club league, with the possibility of one team being obliged to play nine games in 15 days," Lichtenhein explained. "Wanderers will favor a suspension of operations and I understand that the three other clubs, Ottawa, Canadiens and

Quebec, will also favor the same plan. I believe a new league, comprised of Wanderers, Canadiens, Ottawa and Quebec, will be formed and operate this winter.

"The Toronto club claims that the NHA has not kept faith, but the shoe is on the other foot. We informed the Toronto club that we would favor their operating, providing Eddie Livingstone was not connected with the club. We were told that Livingstone's stock would be purchased, but this has not been done. If control of the Toronto club had passed into other hands, Wanderers and Canadiens would have amalgamated, and there would have been a four-club league, comprised of Toronto, Ottawa, Montreal and Quebec."

There was further speculation that the Toronto franchise would be moved to Ottawa and two teams would play out of that city.

"The next move in the professional hockey mix up is up to the Eastern Clubs of the National Hockey Association, as the Toronto Hockey Club will absolutely refuse to retire from the game at the request of the rest of the clubs; and it looks very much like a fight to the finish with the chances about even," the *Ottawa Journal* reported.

The Toronto Hockey Club.

Undaunted, Livingstone proposed a two-team city league in Toronto, one team run by him and one operated by George O'Donoghue, the manager of the amateur Toronto St. Patricks. He also suggested he might organize a rival pro league with teams in Detroit, Cleveland, Hamilton and Pittsburgh, as well as all of the current NHA cities, with plans to raid NHA teams for players.

"The new league is a joke," *Total Hockey* reported Kennedy as saying. "A scream. Just imagine anyone so foolish as to try and operate two teams in Ottawa. And to make jumps between Hamilton and Quebec. The latter is dead and the rink in Hamilton is not big enough."

While things remained uncertain in Eastern Canada, there appeared to be no such consternation out West, where the Patrick brothers, Lester and Frank, felt they could count on nothing but smooth sailing for their league, the PCHA, because they were in control of the entire league.

Whatever front the Patrick brothers put forth, there were nevertheless concerns about the pro game on the West Coast as well. The PCHA was also suffering from a scarcity of quality players tied to enlistment in the war, which led to concerns that the PCHA might be forced to suspend operations. Instead, during the 1917–18 season, the loop dropped its Spokane franchise and went with a three-team outfit.

It was announced in Vancouver on November 9 that the PCHA season would open December 7 with teams in Seattle, Vancouver and Portland. The second half would commence January 22 and wrap up by March 5. Their league champion would then travel eastward to begin the Stanley Cup series against the NHA in mid-March.

Who would be waiting to oppose the PCHA champion remained as uncertain as the conflict in the trenches on the other side of the world.

Soon, that answer would become clearer.

"Revival of NHA Under New Name," screamed the headline

in the November 22, 1917 *Ottawa Citizen*. "Professional Hockey Tangle Will Be Unravelled at Meeting Tonight."

The gathering was actually put off until November 26, but the four clubs that had competed the previous NHA season were all represented at this meeting, held once again in Montreal's Windsor Hotel. Plans were afoot to organize a new four-club league, the only question being: which city would provide the fourth franchise?

It was known for sure that the Montreal Canadiens, Montreal Wanderers and Ottawa Senators were all in. But whether it would be Toronto or Quebec that completed this new loop proved to be the question.

"Quebec have not yet made up their minds regarding the season's plans, but have promised to make known their attitude at this gathering of promoters," the *Montreal Gazette* reported.

"If Quebec decided to drop hockey for this season, Toronto will be given a franchise should they desire to operate one this winter, but it is well known that it must be under entirely different ownership and management to the club operating in the NHA a year ago."

The *Gazette* pointed out that the NHA reserve lists would be recognized by franchises in the new league, and also offered up a couple of interesting tidbits that would prove to be almost prescient.

"It is likely that Frank Calder, who was secretary of the NHA, will be elected president of the new association tonight," it noted, adding that, "only part of the name of the old league will be dropped." Frank Robinson, who'd served as president of the NHA, had already stepped down from that position and given indication that he had no desire to be in charge of any new league. Robinson, it was believed, was appalled by the way the other owners had frozen Livingstone out of the picture.

The *Gazette* reported that hockey's major league would be launched as the National Professional Hockey League.

Rumours were also circulating that the Canadiens and Wanderers were considering amalgamating, talk that apparently was initiated by the Montreal Arena Company and was something that led Kennedy to scoff.

"Wanderers have only one or two players of class to contribute and naturally would not be entitled to an even division of the profits, which is what they ask," Kennedy said.

When Quinn, who'd served as manager of the Quebec team since 1910, tendered his resignation as manager, it was evident that the Bulldogs would not be operating for the 1917–18 season.

Suddenly, Toronto was needed again for the new league to survive. Livingstone was adamant that he would own the team. "My holdings in the Toronto club will be retained by me until such time as I desire to dispose of them, which, I may say, will be the first moment an acceptable offer is submitted and not till then," Livingstone informed the *Toronto Daily News*.

The Montreal Arena Company, which also owned the Toronto rink, was quietly in talks with Livingstone to hammer out some sort of pact that would allow them to operate a Toronto club, though they denied such talk in public.

"It is immaterial to the Montreal Arena whether Toronto is in the Association or not," Montreal Arena manager W.E. Northey told the *Ottawa Journal*. "Personally, I favor a four-club league as being more compact, but that is up to the league, and so long as it is a strong league, it will be able to get dates in Montreal."

A backroom deal was hatched between Livingstone and the Toronto Arena Company to allow them to enter a team in the new NHL using Livingstone's players and installing Mutual Street Arena manager and *Toronto Daily News* columnist Charlie Querrie as manager. The deal called for Livingstone to receive between 50–60 per cent of the profits garnered by the Toronto team during the 1917–18 NHL season.

"The senior hockey league tangle was finally straightened out this afternoon, at a conference of the clubs interested, when the National Hockey League, to take the place of the National Hockey Association of Canada, now suspended, came into existence," the *Ottawa Journal* reported.

"The five clubs which operated in the old body are represented in the new, but only four will operate this season. These four are Ottawa, Toronto, Wanderers and Canadiens of Montreal.

"The Quebec club retains its place on the directorate of the new body, and Mike Quinn, who was named director for the club, has been elected honorary president. Frank Calder, up to the time of its suspension secretary of the old association, was elected to the dual office of president and secretary of the NHL."

Martin Rosenthal (Ottawa), Kennedy, Lichtenhein and Jimmy Murphy (Toronto) were elected to the NHL's board of directors.

"The solution to the difficulties which have beset the senior hockey clubs in their pre-season activities was brought about by the acquisition of the Toronto Hockey Club by a syndicate of Toronto sportsmen, who will place in charge a thoroughly capable manager in James Murphy. Both the new owners and the new manager are acceptable to the other clubs of the league."

In Toronto, the new ownership group was cautioned to distance themselves from Livingstone's past methods of operation. The other NHL owners believed that with Livingstone gone, their fledgling league would thrive.

"Management and conduct of the players have done much to hurt professional hockey in Toronto," the *Ottawa Journal* reported. "Give them the best and the newspapers and the public alike will give pro hockey its just due."

Ottawa's Tommy Gorman described the developments as a "great day for hockey. Livingstone was always arguing. Without him, we can get down to the business of making money."

Kennedy mockingly tipped his cap to his Toronto rival.

"We ought to pass Eddie Livingstone a vote of thanks for solidifying our league," Kennedy said.

Author John Chi-Kit Wong took this backhanded praise of Livingstone one step further in *Lords of the Rinks: The Emergence of the National Hockey League 1875–1936.*

"Livingstone was arguably the most important person in the establishment of the NHL," Wong wrote.

In theory, the NHL was supposed to be a stop-gap measure merely designed so that the other owners could rid themselves of Livingstone, and it was expected that once new owners were in place in Toronto, the teams would return to the NHA.

Instead, the Toronto Arena group opted to stiff Livingstone, not living up to their end of the agreement, refusing to pay him his cut of the profits from the 1917–18 season and then signing the players to contracts with them for the 1918–19 season.

Livingstone sued the NHL, but on February 28, 1918, his case was dismissed in a Toronto court. Livingstone immediately launched an appeal.

"Eddie Livingstone, ex-magnate of Toronto, has had his little experience with the Law Horrible, and said experience will cost him about $1,000, which is a lot of money in war time," noted the *Ottawa Journal*. But it may be worth a thousand to Eddie to learn that when in professional sport, he should do as other magnates do. Also, that he shouldn't monkey with the machinery.

"There have been worse owners than Livingstone in professional hockey. Eddie had his faults, plenty of them, a principal one that he was too willing to rush into print and into conversation with troubles that might have been adjusted quite easily before they were magnified by undue publicity into greater proportions than they should have been.

"A little more diplomacy and Edward might still have been in professional hockey."

When Livingstone's rival league, dubbed the Canadian Hockey Association, failed to get off the ground, he sought to reorganize the NHA, recruiting owners from long-lost NHA franchises to reappear at the NHL's annual meeting prior to the 1918–19 season. Unable to easily eliminate Livingstone from the equation, on December 11th, 1918, the NHA was officially dissolved.

After a decade of courtroom dealings, Livingstone finally won his court case against the NHL in 1927. He was awarded $5,000 for lost profits and $10,000 for the loss of his hockey team.

By 1927, the NHL was a rollicking 10-team juggernaut with two divisions and clubs in major U.S. centres like New York, Boston, Detroit and Chicago. Raking in the cash, the cost to finally be rid of Livingstone would have been viewed as money well spent.

MINUTES OF THE FIRST NHL MEETING

At a meeting of representatives of hockey clubs held at the Windsor Hotel, Montreal, the following present, G.W. Kendall, S.E. Lichtenhein, T.P. Gorman, M.J. Quinn and Frank Calder, it was explained by the last named that in view of the suspension of operations by the National Hockey Association of Canada Limited, he had called the meeting at the suggestion of the Quebec Hockey Club to ascertain if some steps could not be taken to perpetuate the game of hockey.

Frank Calder was elected to the Chair and a discussion ensued after which it was moved by T.P. Gorman, seconded by G.W. Kendall: "That the Canadiens, Wanderers, Ottawa and Quebec Hockey Clubs unite to comprise the National Hockey League." The motion was carried.

It was then moved by M.J. Quinn seconded by G.W. Kendall that: "This League agrees to operate under the rules and conditions governing the game of hockey prescribed by the National Hockey Association of Canada Limited." The motion was carried.

At this stage, Mr. W.E. Northey, representing the Toronto Arena Company, asked to be admitted to the meeting and was admitted. Mr. Northey explained that he was empowered by the interests he represented to say that in the event of a league being formed to contain four clubs, the Toronto Arenas desired to enter a team in the competition.

Upon this assurance M.J. Quinn on behalf of the Quebec Hockey Club declared the latter willing to withdraw provided a suitable arrangement could be made regarding players, then the property of the Quebec Hockey Club.

After discussion, it was unanimously agreed that the Quebec players be taken over by the league at a cost of $700 of which amount 50% should be paid to the Quebec Hockey Club by the club winning the championship, 30% by the second club and 20% by the third club in the race.

The meeting then proceeded to the election of officers. The following directors were elected S.E. Lichtenhein (Wanderers), Martin Rosenthal (Ottawa), G.W. Kendall (Canadiens) and a director to be named by the Toronto club.

M.J. Quinn was elected Honorary President with power to vote on matters pertaining to the general welfare of the league.

Frank Calder was elected President and Secretary-Treasurer at a salary of $800 on the understanding that there could be no appeal from his decisions.

After a schedule of Wednesday and Saturday games was adopted the meeting was adjourned.

From the Minutes of the First NHL Board of Governors Meeting November 26, 1917

HOW THEY
PLAYED THE GAME

Pro hockey was barely a decade old when the NHL's first season got underway in the winter of 1917, and in some circles, the professional game was still viewed with a healthy skepticism by some, especially in the Toronto area, where the influence of Ontario Hockey Association president and Toronto Telegram publisher John Ross Robertson, the champion of the amateur game, continued to rule with an iron fist.

Toronto was the pre-eminent force in Canadian amateur hockey. The Toronto Dentals were the reigning Allan Cup holders as champions of senior hockey, and in this era, the Allan Cup competition was looked upon with reverence equal to that of the Stanley Cup. The Memorial Cup would be introduced to be presented to the Canadian junior champions, and the first winner would also be from the GTA, with the University of Toronto Schools taking home the trophy.

It didn't help matters that in Toronto, the pro game often devolved into a sideshow due to the bombastic ways of Toronto franchise owner Eddie Livingstone. The constant petty infighting among the people who ran pro hockey often gave that brand of the game a black eye, and fans in some centres still preferred the so-called purity of the amateur game to the paid brand of hockey.

Not that the pros were pulling in the kind of salaries that today's millionaire NHLers garner. Montreal captain Newsy Lalonde, among the best players in the league, pulled down $1,300 for the 1917–18 season, which would equate to about $25,000 in current Canadian funds. NHL president Frank Calder garnered a salary of $800.

The average height of an original NHLer was 5–8 and the average player weighed in around 173 pounds.

The type of hockey put on display by NHL clubs in 1917 would hardly be recognizable to someone familiar with the game as it is played today.

First of all, there were no lines on the ice beyond the two goal lines that intersected from one goalpost to the other in each net. The only other marking on the ice was the centre ice dot for faceoffs. The blue lines weren't added to the rink until the 1918–19 season.

You also would have never seen a Zamboni. Frank Zamboni wouldn't invent his ice-cleaning machine until the 1940s and in these days, crews of ice cleaners with shovels would work diligently to clear the rink of snow during inter-missions. The arena sound system was often a band playing the popular tunes of the day.

The arenas themselves were as different and unique as the game of 1917 was compared to the current brand of NHL hockey. Toronto's Mutual Street Arena was the largest in the league, with an ice surface measuring 230 x 95 feet and room for 7,000 fans. It was also the only artificial ice surface in the NHL.

Ottawa's Dey's Arena, also known as the Laurier Ave. Arena, held 7,000 with an ice surface measuring 200 x 81. It's circular shape—most early ice surfaces were rectangular—helped to popularize a play that continues today, players rimming the puck around the boards.

Montreal's Westmount Arena was the first hockey-specific rink to be constructed in Canada. It only sat 4,000, but with standing room could accommodate up to 7,000 spectators, and its ice surface of 200 x 85 continues as the NHL standard to this day. Also a circular ice surface, another feature of the Westmount Arena that's become an NHL standard were the four-foot boards that encase the ice rink, allowing players to develop another popular hockey tactic that remains today, the chipping of the puck off the boards to get past an opponent.

When fire destroyed the Westmount Arena on January 2, 1918, the Montreal Wanderers opted to drop from the NHL, while co-tenants, the Montreal Canadiens, returned to their old home at the Jubilee Rink, which was half the size of the Westmount Arena and sat just 3,200.

Playing their first game there against Ottawa on January 5, 1918, the Canadiens competed in borrowed equipment and sweaters from the Hochelaga team of the Montreal City League, having lost all their gear in the flames of the Westmount fire.

Perhaps most strangely of all to a modern observer, forward passing of the puck was completely prohibited, making the most valuable players those slick, speedy puckhandlers who were capable of deking and dazzling their way through the opposition to put it singlehandedly in the net. Players such as Montreal Canadiens stars Newsy Lalonde and Joe Malone were especially adept at such manoeuvres. Hockey of this era was a skating, stickhandling game. Passing was so passé that

Joe Malone.

51

the NHL didn't even bother to officially tabulate assists during the 1917–18 season.

Indeed, most viewed the passing of the puck to be lazy hockey. It was felt that it took skill to beat someone one-on-one and that's how the game should be played.

For that reason, some of the stat lines of the top players during the 1917–18 season read more like the won-lost record of a superstar baseball pitcher. Malone topped the NHL scoring race with 44 goals and only four assists. Following Malone in the scoring race was Ottawa's Cy Denneny (36–10), Toronto's Reg Noble (30–10), Montreal's Lalonde (23–7) and Toronto's Corb Denneny (20–9).

Player substitutions were completed in vastly different fashion during the NHL's infancy. Beyond the starting six on the ice, there were no other forward lines or defensive pairings. Teams did not work in shifts, as they do now in the modern era.

Some of the brighter, forward-thinking minds felt many of these measures were draconian and detrimental to the growth of hockey, that the game's pace would increase dramatically with freer substitution.

Forwards would average 40 or more minutes of ice time per game, while defencemen, who with few exceptions rarely got involved in the rush during this era, would see upwards of 50 minutes playing time per night. It wasn't uncommon for some players to spend the entire game on the ice. In fact, during a January 5, 1918 overtime game against the Montreal Canadiens, Ottawa Senators player-manager Eddie Gerard never left the ice during the complete 77:15 contest.

At some rinks, the extra players didn't even occupy the bench. In Ottawa, where the natural ice surface required the arena temperature to be maintained at an extremely frigid level, spare players often took refuge in the steam-heated dressing room, where some would play cards to pass the time. A buzzer system was rigged up from the bench, and when the coach felt a sub was required, he'd ring the buzzer, a player would emerge and soon enter the fray.

Positional play was also still evolving. It had only been a few years since the role of the defencemen had been altered to where they were situated side by side on the ice. Previously, these two players had been labelled the point and the cover point, and they were positioned one in front of the other, the cover point serving as the last line of defence in front of the netminder.

Forwards and defencemen also weren't allowed to kick the puck, although the prohibitions placed upon them were nothing compared to the limitations placed on goaltenders.

To start, a goalie couldn't freeze the puck to stop play. Nor were netminders permitted to pass the puck to a teammate. And they were prohibited from leaving their feet to make a save, an act that was punishable by a two-minute penalty.

This certainly explains the inflated goals-against averages of the 1917–18 season. Canadiens netminder Georges Vezina led the way at 3.93, which was actually quite a spectacular number considering the limited stopping options available to these early netminders. Toronto's Harry (Hap) Holmes (4.73) and Ottawa's Clint Benedict (5.12) were second and third best.

As if their lives weren't already difficult enough, when goaltenders were penalized, they were required to serve their own infractions, and there were no requirements to have back-up netminders in uniform, so if a goalie was called for a foul and sent to the penalty box, a teammate would be required to guard the net. And in 1917–18, minor penalties were three minutes in length.

Montreal Wanderers player-manager Art Ross, considered one of the smartest people in hockey, felt that goalies should

Georges Vezina.

be allowed to stop the puck in any manner of their choosing. "Let them bite the puck, if necessary," Ross said. He also thought goalies should be permitted to pass the puck up ice to teammates and that players should be permitted to kick the puck. It wouldn't be long before the moguls running the game would agree with him.

On January 9, 1918, NHL president Frank Calder decreed the first major rule change in league history when he cleared the way for netminders to go down. NHL goalers had been dropping like flies in front of pucks in the early games of the season, but even though this tactic was forbidden by the rules, referees had proved reluctant to penalize these goalies.

"Both [Clint] Benedict and [Bert] Lindsay were warned for getting on their knees, but were allowed to go unpenalized, although they offended several times," reported the *Toronto World* of an early season Ottawa-Wanderers game.

Finally, Calder decided he'd heard enough complaining, both from goalies who felt they were being unfairly restricted in their puck-stopping abilities, and from game officials frustrated with trying to determine whether the goaltender fell deliberately or accidentally in front of a shot. By making this change, he also brought the regulations governing how netminders in the NHL were permitted to stop the puck in line with the rules already in place within the Pacific Coast Hockey Association, the NHL's major-league rival for the Stanley Cup.

"In the future, they can fall on their knees or stand on their heads, if they think they can stop the puck better in that way than by standing on their feet," Calder said, in the process, coining a phrase that remains part of the hockey vernacular today as a method of describing spectacular netminding.

The main culprit was Senators goalie Benedict, mockingly known as Praying Benny and Tumbling Clint because he spent so much time on his knees. Benedict admitted that he liked to keep the referee guessing as to his intent when he went down.

"What you had to be is sneaky," Benedict explained to the *Montreal Star*. "You'd make a move, fake losing your balance or footing, and put the officials on the spot—did I fall down, or did I intentionally go down?"

Calder insisted that Benedict's sneaky strategy was not behind the decision to change the rulebook mid-season. "Of course, the idea is not to favour Ottawa, or any other one club," Calder said. "But to help the entire league, the public, the teams and the officials.

"Very few of the teams carry a spare netminder, and if the goaler is ruled off, it means a long delay in equipping another player, and in a close contest, would undoubtedly cost the penalized team the game. The old rule made it hard for the referees, so everybody will be helped."

Speaking of the officials, they were quite different than what you see on the ice today. With no lines, there was no need for linesman. Officiating crews were two-man units consisting of a referee, who was in charge of the game, and an assistant referred to as a judge of play, although both were eligible to call penalties. Some of the officials were past stars of the game like Harvey Pulford, once a defenceman with the legendary Ottawa Silver Seven and a four-time Stanley Cup champion, and Jack

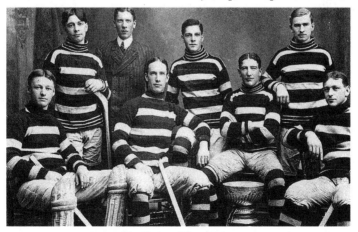

The Ottawa Silver Seven.

Marshall, a forward who won six Stanley Cup titles with four different teams as a player.

Others came from different backgrounds. Lou Marsh was a sportswriter with the *Toronto Telegram* who would often officiate a game and also write a story for his paper about the contest. It's a safe bet that he never criticized the work of the officials in his write ups.

There was no such thing as a power play in the NHL of this era. In the case of a penalty, the opposition was immediately allowed to substitute for the penalized player, so they were never required to play shorthanded. If a team drew so many penalties at the same time as to not be able to put five skaters on the ice in front of their netminder, the opposition team was required to remove players from the ice until the two teams were at even strength.

There was talk of introducing a delayed penalty rule during the season, but it was determined to defer that decision until after the season ended. The NHL moguls also felt there was no need for a red light behind the net to signify a goal, as was suggested by some in the hockey world as a way of making it easier for fans around the rink to know that the puck was in the net.

With so little in terms of regulatory measures on the ice left to impact play, stoppages generally only resulted from goals, pucks going out of play, or penalty calls.

That led to a humorous moment during a February 20, 1918 contest between the Canadiens and Toronto. The levity was supplied by Canadiens defenceman Joe Hall. Nicknamed Bad Joe for his rugged and often illegal style of play, after a Toronto player fell over his stick, Hall, who would lead the league with 100 penalty minutes, instinctively skated over and sat down in the penalty box. When Canadiens captain Newsy Lalonde demanded to know what infraction Hall had committed, referee Marshall informed Lalonde he'd called no foul and Hall was merely penalized by a guilty conscience. Hall sheepishly skated back onto the ice. "Sorry, Newsy," Hall said. "Force of habit."

Joe Hall.

While the NHL was slow and often resistant to change, something that hasn't changed much over the 100-year history of the league, the Pacific Coast Hockey Association, the NHL's major-league rival and the loop that they would face off with for the Stanley Cup at the conclusion of each league's playoffs, was quick to adapt and experiment with different measures if they thought it could improve the game.

The PCHA had already implemented many of the measures that the NHL was still pondering, and fans would be offered the chance each spring to decide which brand of hockey they preferred, since during Stanley Cup play the games would be alternated between each league's rule book.

In PCHA games, forward passing was allowed, making its brand of hockey a much faster-paced game. They were the first league to put numbers on the back of players' sweaters to aid fans in identifying them on the ice. Blue lines marked the PCHA ice surface, assists were awarded and delayed penalties were served, leading to the first power plays. The PCHA was also the first major pro league to introduce the penalty shot. And not only could PCHA netminders drop and flop to stop the puck, it wasn't uncommon to see goalers like Vancouver's Hugh Lehman race from his net, corral a loose biscuit and send a pass sailing up to one of his forwards. The PCHA was also the first to implement a playoff system. The PCHA expanded into U.S. markets when Portland, Oregon was awarded a franchise in 1914, a decade before the Boston Bruins would become the NHL's first American-based franchise. That same year, the Patricks established the Boundary Hockey League in British Columbia, the first minor-league feeder system. In the mid-1920s, Lester Patrick would become the first coach to begin alternating set forward lines and changing them on the fly. The frenetic pace they were able to establish via this quick-change artistry simply wore down the NHL champion Montreal Canadiens as Lester Patrick guided the Victoria Cougars to the 1924–25 Stanley Cup title, the last team to win the Cup from outside the NHL.

Curiously, though, the PCHA held steadfast to seven-man hockey, maintaining the rover position, a spot dropped by the NHA back in 1911, for more than a decade after it became passé elsewhere. Eastern hockey people felt that seven players on each team clogged up the ice too much, but the PCHA continued to ice the rover until 1923.

There was a distinct advantage that the PCHA held over the NHL. The league was owned and operated entirely by the Patrick brothers, Frank and Lester. They backed the league financially with the millions their father Joe earned in the British Columbia lumber industry and controlled all the franchises. Players signed their contracts with the Patricks and not with the teams for which they played.

It was, in a sense, a dictatorship, with the Patricks deciding how their game would be played. While the flamboyant, talkative Lester—a dapper dresser who naturally attracted attention to himself—gained most of the notoriety from the PCHA, it was actually Frank who was the brainchild behind many of the league's innovations.

Running their own ship without the requirement of answering to a board of directors, the Patricks could alter and control the game at their leisure, and discipline was handled in similar fashion. When Seattle's Cully Wilson severely injured Vancouver's Mickey MacKay with a cross-check to the face in a game during a February 26, 1919 game, he was fined $500 and expelled from the PCHA for the 1919–20 season. The differing philosophies of the two leagues were emphasized when Wilson immediately signed to play for Toronto and led the NHL in penalty minutes during the 1919–20 campaign.

Unlike the Patricks, NHL president Frank Calder had no such dictatorial powers, and the players understood this. Violent play was more frequent in the early years of the NHL.

Respect for authority was also lacking in the NHL. During a January 26 game, Toronto defenceman Harry Mummery got into a disagreement with an Ottawa police officer when he pursued a fan who called him a vile name as he left the ice at the end of the second period. Mummery later sought out the policeman and apologized for his actions.

The violence between the Toronto and Canadiens clubs reared up again in January. In the dying moments of a 5–1 Toronto victory on January 28, Montreal's Joe Hall bodychecked Toronto's Alf Skinner, who had just returned to the ice after serving a penalty for butt-ending Hall in the chin. Skinner retaliated by jabbing Hall with the blade of his stick, then swinging his stick at Hall's head, cutting Hall open and smashing three of his teeth. Hall retaliated and clouted Skinner over the head with his stick, rendering the Toronto player unconscious.

After the game, both players were arrested by Toronto police and charged with common assault. Querrie showed up, posted $100 bond for each, and bailed both players out of jail.

Hall and Skinner appeared in court the next day and both pleaded guilty to disorderly conduct. Magistrate Ellis fined each man $15 and gave them suspended sentences. "My officers say that Hall was more to blame than Skinner," Toronto police inspector McKinney explained. "We must have clean sport here, and the police intend to see that it is kept clean and will back up officials when they strive for this end, and when they fail, we will step in."

Hall and Skinner decided to let bygones be bygones and left the courthouse walking arm in arm. But Canadiens manager George Kennedy accused the Toronto police of interference with the game and bias in favour of the home team. "The officers didn't want to arrest Skinner at first," Kennedy claimed to the *Toronto World*. "But when I said I would personally get a warrant, they decided to take Skinner as well as Hall, and that put an end to the possibility of Hall getting a court sentence, for it was obvious that Skinner was equally to blame."

On February 2 when the same teams met at the Jubilee Rink, Montreal fans chanted for Hall to get Skinner in retaliation for their altercation in Toronto and one rowdy spectator threw a full gin bottle in Skinner's direction. Players insisted the area on the ice where the bottle landed gave off the scent of a distillery. Montreal forward Didier Pitre pointed the fan out to arena security and he was apprehended and removed from the premises by Montreal police.

A February 16 Ottawa-Canadiens game also deteriorated into mayhem, highlighted by a toe-to-toe fight between Ottawa's Cy Denneny and Montreal's Bert Corbeau. Unhappy with a penalty called against him, Canadiens defenceman Hall hurled his stick down the ice and was assessed a major foul. Sitting out a penalty, Ottawa's Harry Hyland got

Harry Hyland.

into a dispute with nearby fans and left the penalty bench to scrap with them, his teammates charging across the ice to join in the fray. Police intervened to separate the combatants. A squad of police guarded the route to the Ottawa dressing room at game's end.

Of all the miscreants in the wild west setting that was the NHL in its infancy, Toronto captain Ken Randall was the most ornery. Often referred to as the stormy petrel of the league, a person who thrived on conflict, the only thing Randall did more than cause trouble was to refuse to take responsibility for his actions.

On the eve of Toronto's big February 23 showdown with Ottawa, the loser of which would likely be eliminated from the playoff race, the NHL suspended the Toronto captain for using abusive and threatening language toward referee Lou Marsh during the club's previous game. It was the fourth occasion during the season that Randall had been fined for abusing referees and he'd yet to pay any of his fines. NHL president Calder informed Randall he wouldn't be allowed to play again until he paid up.

"I am sorry for Randall, who is a good fellow off the ice, but too hot tempered," Calder said. "But our officials must be protected at any cost, and on the basis of referee Marsh's report, there was no other step to to take.

"It will serve as a warning to other players, too."

When Randall was assessed a $25 fine for cross-checking Canadiens goalie Georges Vezina into his net and then sassing the officials when he was called for the penalty during a February 20 game, Calder finally opted to take a stand. The NHL president decreed that until Randall paid his fines—now totalling $35—he would be suspended indefinitely. The battle between league rules and rule breaker came to a humorous end prior to that February 23 game.

Randall skated out and presented $32 in bills and $3 in pennies in a paper bag to referee Lou Marsh, whose report had led to

Randall's suspension, the first in NHL history. Marsh declined to accept the bag of pennies, so Randall laid the paper sack down at the referee's feet and skated away.

Ottawa's Harry Hyland, anxious to start the game, swatted the bag of coppers with his stick, spilling them all over the ice, and a squadron of young boys poured over the boards, gleefully grabbing up the loose change.

Eventually, a sheepish Randall retired to the dressing room, gathered up $3 in bills and brought them back to Marsh so that he could play and the game could begin.

Discipline had eventually won the day. Perhaps there was hope for the NHL as a major league after all.

THE ORIGINALS: THE TEAMS

The debate over how many teams would suit up during the NHL's first season was one that very nearly scuttled the season entirely.

It had been universally agreed that only four teams would, but just which four teams would make up the first NHL season, but just which four teams would prove to be contentious virtually right up until the November 26, 1917 day that the league was officially born.

Toronto, the franchise that had been suspended by the NHA during the 1916–17 season, was originally supposed to be excluded, but then Quebec ran into roster difficulties. There was brief talk of two teams in Ottawa, and also speculation that the two Montreal teams, the Wanderers and the Canadiens, would be folded into one.

When the puck first dropped on the NHL's initial campaign on December 19, 1917, five teams comprised the league, though only four were active franchises.

MONTREAL CANADIENS

Formed in 1909, one of the founding members of the NHA, two-time defending NHA champions, as well as Stanley Cup

The Montreal Canadiens.

champions in 1915–16, the Canadiens came into the NHL's first season looking to be in the best shape of any of the teams in the league.

The lineup included six players from their 1915–16 Cup winner—goalie Georges Vezina, defenceman Bert Corbeau and forwards Newsy Lalonde, Didier Pitre, Jack Laviolette and Louis Berlinquette. To that was added two more Cup winners from Quebec in forward Joe Malone, who shared the NHA goal-scoring lead with 41 in 1916–17, and veteran rearguard Joe Hall, considered among the toughest customers in pro hockey.

"Canadiens are strengthened about 40 per cent with the addition of Malone and Hall," wrote Elmer Ferguson in the *Montreal Herald*. "Canadiens will take a lot of beating, barring accidents and unlucky breaks."

The *Ottawa Journal* agreed with Ferguson's assessment. "Malone, Lalonde and Pitre ... look the best scoring outfit in the league. [They are] a forward line that does not need a million chances each game to score six or seven goals."

It certainly started out as the pundits predicted. The Canadiens opened the campaign 9–2 and won the first half NHL title, assuring a place in the playoff for the league championship. But soon after, cracks began to appear in Montreal's armour.

An older team with eight players in their 30s, the firewagon hockey made famous by the Canadiens was not as evident. "Canadiens are the Flying Frenchmen no longer," noted the *Toronto Mail and Empire.* "A few seasons ago very few teams would have stopped them by superior speed and persistent backchecking.

"Things have changed, and with their speed gone, Canadiens are trying to win games by their grey matter."

The Canadiens won only five of their last 12 games, finishing the regular season on a three-game losing streak, and fell 10–7 to Toronto in the two-game total goals NHL championship series.

A century later, the Canadiens remain the only team to remain in the NHL since Day 1 without a change in location or name. They've added 23 Stanley Cups since becoming a charter member of the league, far and away the most of any NHL team, and were the only NHL team to win the Stanley Cup in every decade from the 1910s–1990s.

MONTREAL WANDERERS

One of the most famous teams in the sport, charting the history of the Wanderers involves a who's who of hockey heritage.

It was actually Wanderers' manager Jimmy Gardner in 1909 who suggested to J. Ambrose O'Brien that he put together a team of French-Canadian players to serve as foil to the English-speaking supporters of the Wanderers and join the newly formed NHA. That idea spawned the birth of the Montreal Canadiens.

So many of the game's early greats wore the Wanderers' famous white sweater with the red band around the middle.

James Strachan, who'd later serve as president of the NHL's Montreal Maroons, was an original Wanderer in 1904–05. Lester and Frank Patrick skated for the Wanderers, as did Bruce and Hod

The Montreal Wanderers.

Stuart, the latter considered the greatest player in the history of the game at the time. Riley Hern, considered hockey's first great puck-stopper, tended goal for the team's three successive Stanley Cup triumphs from 1905–06 to 1907–08. By 1917, Hern worked as a goal judge at NHL games, and operated one of the most popular and fashionable haberdasheries in Montreal. His store manager was none other than Wanderers forward Jack McDonald.

As legendary as their status was, by the birth of the NHL, all the Wanderers had going for them was brave talk and glorious memories. They'd been a losing team in three of their last four NHA seasons, including a disastrous 5–15 in 1916–17.

On November 8, 1917, legendary hockey man Art Ross was named player-manager of Wanderers, replacing Dickie Boon, who resigned due to conflicts with his business interests. Boon and Strachan were partners in a coal company.

"Wanderers will have a much stronger team than last year," team president Sam Lichtenhein vowed to the *Ottawa Journal*. "We are out after four more players, two of them amateurs and two professionals.

"We will not only have a strong team, but we will be on the ice earlier than any other team in the Association. We will hold our first practice on November 26. We will get ice at the Arena if we can and if we can't then we will rent elsewhere. But we will turn out on November 26, if there is ice to be secured.

"All the players are full of confidence. I think Ross will be a good leader, particularly useful in developing the younger players. I think the Wanderers will be well up in the race this year."

Lichtenhein was also determined that his team be a patriotic bunch and support the war effort. "I am strong for patriotic hockey and I am not going to have any players on my team this winter who are not helping the cause in some way," Lichtenhein told the *Winnipeg Tribune*. "All my players must, in addition to playing hockey, assist their country in their great war in some manner, unless they are married men."

Cecil Hart, the publicity man for the Wanderers, was another who would become famous in Montreal hockey circles. Hart would later be named the original manager of the Montreal Maroons when they joined the NHL in 1924. After leaving the Maroons, Hart would be named coach of the Canadiens, guiding the Habs to successive Stanley Cup titles in 1929–30 and 1930–31, and making him the only man to serve with all three of Montreal's NHL clubs. It was Hart's father, Dr. David A. Hart, who donated the Hart Trophy, presented annually to the NHL's most valuable player since 1924.

Though the Wanderers were confident that their fortunes would turn around in the new league, it wasn't a confidence shared by those outside their circle.

"The Red Bands will cop this winter," player-manager Art Ross boldly claimed prior to the start of the 1917–18 NHL season, to which the *Ottawa Journal* responded, "We take it, however, that Art only means the Red Bands will cop the poker games."

There were those who took umbrage at this widespread jocularity at the Wanderers' expense.

"A story sent out from Montreal declares Wanderers look weaker this season than for a great many years, which is a deliberate and malicious representation of facts," the *Montreal Herald* reported. "Wanderers now look far better than at the start of last year, with their new Quebec material and the promising amateurs which are being tried out.

"The same story—which oddly enough was not published in Montreal—says the amateurs working out with the red bands have no intention of turning pro but such is not the case. Those who can make the grade will be glad to jump."

Among the amateurs trying out were forwards Jerry Geran and Raymie Skilton. Americans up from Boston, they were in Canada offering their expertise to help modernize munitions plants and aid the war effort. When first Geran and then Skilton played for the Wanderers, they became the NHL's first American-born and trained players.

The bold talk from the Wanderers' training camp quickly turned to bleak reality. Star defenceman Sprague Cleghorn was lost to a broken leg before the season started. His brother, forward Odie Cleghorn, was declared unfit for military service and therefore ruled ineligible to play hockey.

Goaltending was also a huge concern for the team. "Wanderers are shy of high-class netminding material," the *Ottawa Journal* noted. There was speculation they would pursue Quebec goalie Paddy Moran, a two-time Stanley Cup winner who was close friends with Ross. Veteran pros Billy Hague and Bert Lindsay, former Wanderer Albert Leblanc and amateur Dick Dooner from Loyola College all tried out during training camp.

Goaltending wasn't their only worry. "Wanderers are short of forwards says manager Art Ross," reported the *Ottawa Journal*. "Looks like Art will be forced to use army artillery to get goals."

The Wanderers, once proud warriors, continued to be the butt of jokes.

"Sammy Lichtenhein drafted three Quebec players," the *Ottawa Journal* reported after the dispersal draft of the dormant Bulldogs franchise. "But 'darn the luck,' says Sammy, 'they want to claim [military] exemption.'"

The Wanderers would get off to a smashing start, outscoring Toronto at home by a 10–9 count to win the NHL's first game. But only 700 showed up to watch what would also be their last win.

After losing their next three games by a combined score of 26–9, the Wanderers folded on January 3, 1918, the day after Montreal's Westmount Arena burnt to the ground, taking all of the team's equipment with it. Some of the Wanderers players were dispersed to the other NHL teams.

"The defaulting of the Wanderers will mark the passing of one of the best-known clubs in the hockey world," the *Toronto World* noted.

"Thousands will regret the passing of the famous Redbands, who have been honourably connected with the great winter sport for many years and will hope to see them come back next winter," the *Ottawa Citizen* reported.

They wouldn't be back. The Wanderers were done. They would wander the ice no more.

OTTAWA SENATORS

The history of hockey in Ottawa and the origins of this franchise draw well back into the days before there ever was a Stanley Cup. Ottawa's first club team was formed in 1883 and a decade later, it was Ottawa that was vanquished by the Montreal Amateur Athletic Association in the first Stanley Cup game.

Ottawa's Silver Seven—a nicknamed granted to the team after a local druggist awarded each of them a silver nugget— won Ottawa's first Stanley Cup and defended the title nine times between 1903–06, in the days when any team could put forth a challenge for the Stanley Cup to its trustees. If deemed a worthy challenge, the champions were required to defend the trophy as soon as dates for the games could be arranged.

The Senators were founding members of the NHA in 1909, bringing Ottawa into pro hockey, and they won back-to-back

The Ottawa Senators.

Stanley Cup titles in 1908–09 and 1909–10, the first as members of the Eastern Canada Amateur Hockey Association and the second as pros in the inaugural NHA campaign.

Defenceman Hamby Shore, who was still with the Senators as they broke into the NHL in 1917–18, was part of the 1909–10 Cup championship squad.

No NHL club was hit as hard with player losses due to the breakout of the Great War as was the Senators. Angus Duford, Punch Broadbent and Leth Graham all enlisted in the Canadian military and saw combat duty. Graham was a victim of a poison gas attack and although he returned to play in the NHL post war, he was never capable of being more than a spare player. Defenceman Morley Bruce was conscripted during the 1917–18 season, as was forward Harry Hyland.

Georges Boucher had also attempted to enlist overseas but was rejected because of his bum knee, the same knee that he'd injured playing football and had left him under the care of a physician as the Senators opened training camp in late November.

Meanwhile, centre Frank Nighbor, who shared the NHL scoring lead with 41 goals in 1916–17, was also out of action, stationed in Toronto as a mechanic with the Royal Flying Corps. Nighbor was expected to train in Texas with Royal

Flying Corps and it appeared doubtful that he'd see any action on his skates this season.

"Frank Nighbor might avoid Newsy Lalonde's swinging stick this winter by bringing along his aeroplane and flying from goal to goal," joked the *Ottawa Journal.*

When the Ottawa team opened training, the roster included player-manager Eddie Gerard, goalie Clint Benedict, Boucher, forwards Jack Darragh, Cy Denneny, Eddie Lowrey, and defenceman Bruce. Bill Mooney, a defenceman from the Ottawa Royal Canadians seniors, was also trying out and was expected to sign in a few days.

"[Veteran defenceman] Doc Merrill has positively announced that he will not play and Hamby Shore has named terms that the club cannot meet," the *Ottawa Journal* reported. "It is not known whether Georges Boucher will be able to play because of his knee [injured playing football] and Nighbor is also uncertain, as he may be overseas by Christmas. If not, he will play in the home games at least."

Not surprisingly, the weakened Senators were unable to match up with the more powerful Toronto and Montreal Canadiens clubs. It didn't help matters when several players got into a contract squabble with the team's owners, insisting on a raise because the schedule had been increased from 20 to 24 games. The impasse delayed the start of Ottawa's home opener against the Canadiens. Darragh spent the first period of the season renegotiating his deal and didn't suit up until the first intermission.

Ottawa opened with consecutive losses, surrendering 18 goals in the process. The Senators won just two of their first seven games and three of their first 10, finishing the first half in third place with a 5–9 slate.

One of the problems with the Senators was that they couldn't match the physicality of the rugged Toronto and Canadiens teams. Ottawa's squad was mockingly referred to as a "pink tea bunch."

There was hope that the second half would be better. Nighbor had obtained a leave from the Royal Flying Corps and was finally available, and Hyland had given the team a proven scorer and a veteran presence when he was added from the defunct Montreal Wanderers.

Playing manager Gerard named the feisty Hyland his assistant coach, and the move seemed to give the Senators a boost.

"Hibernian Harry Hyland seems to be just the party needed to put into the Ottawa hockey team the old fighting aggressive spirit, which seems to have been its only lacking asset," the *Montreal Herald* noted. "Hyland would fight [world heavyweight champion] Jess Willard if he thought the champ was trying to slip something over on him."

When Ottawa opened the second half with a solid 6–3 triumph over the first half champion Canadiens, the hope that things would be different grew exponentially. But that hope quickly faded. The Senators lost their next three games and any hopes of a second-half crown were gone.

Denneny was second in the NHL in scoring with 36 goals and 46 points, but found little in the way of support. Only three other Senators hit double digits in goals and no other player netted more than 14 times. Ottawa allowed a league-high 114 goals against.

Soon enough, however, Ottawa would be the scourge of the league. The Senators would form the NHL's first dynasty, winning Stanley Cups in 1919–20, 1920–21 and 1922–23. Players from this club, including Denneny, Nighbor, Gerard, Darragh, Boucher, Benedict, and Broadbent, returning from combat duty, formed the nucleus of this championship run. The Senators would win another Cup in 1926–27, but by then the NHL landscape was changing.

With major American cities such as Boston, New York, Detroit and Chicago on board, the NHL was a thriving 10-team league. Salaries were blossoming and a small-market Ottawa club with a tiny, outdated rink could not compete. Desperate to survive, Ottawa began dealing off top players like Hooley Smith and King Clancy to create cash flow.

The Senators made their last playoff appearance in 1929–30. In 1931, with the Great Depression raging, Ottawa took a one-season leave of absence from the NHL in order to try and get out of debt. The NHL co-signed a loan to bring Ottawa back into the loop in 1932, but the Senators were a last-place team in 1932–33. Under new management the following season, Ottawa again finished in the basement and prior to the 1934 season the franchise was relocated to St. Louis. Ottawa would not return to the NHL until 1992, when the current version of the Senators was born.

QUEBEC BULLDOGS

Like the Montreal Wanderers, the Bulldogs were a once-mighty club that had fallen on hard times. Stanley Cup champions in 1911–12 and 1912–13, several players from those teams—forwards Joe Malone, Jack McDonald, Jack Marks and Rusty Crawford and defencemen Joe Hall and Harry Mummery—were still part of the club.

The Bulldogs desperately tried to ice a team for the 1917–18 season, but the obstacles proved too much. A shortage of players led

The Quebec Bulldogs.

Bulldogs manager Mike Quinn to seek a merger with the Quebec Sons of Ireland, who'd captured the Ross Cup title as senior hockey champions of Quebec in 1915–16 and 1916–17. Though the team included on its roster future NHLers such as Art Gagne, Frank Brophy and George McNaughton, at the time there was no mutual interest from the amateur stars to seek out a pro career.

Financing proved another roadblock, so Quinn began knocking on prominent doors in search of investors. The owners of the Quebec Arena didn't have the funds to operate the club. Quinn met with Arthur Drapeau, a well-known theatrical entrepreneur, but Drapeau insisted that his many business interests made it impossible for him to operate a pro hockey team.

When the NHL was formed on November 26, 1917, the Bulldogs joined the league but then took a leave of absence and temporarily suspended operations. Their players were loaned to the other four NHL clubs via a dispersal draft.

"The team that lands Harry Mummery this winter will have no need to fear beefless days," joked the *Ottawa Journal* of the portly Quebec defenceman, who was known to devour a steak, a pie and a pint of cream as a pre-game meal.

Quinn asked $200 per player as a loan fee, but was informed that the Quebec club would only get money from teams that turned a profit during the season.

"The suspension may be a good thing for the game in Quebec, and when next season comes around the hockey public may be less apathetic and more enthusiastic, thus encouraging some of the younger element to go ahead and put Quebec on the pro hockey map again," the *Ottawa Journal* felt.

Quebec would play one game during the NHL's inaugural campaign, an exhibition contest on February 2, 1918, in Quebec City. The Montreal Canadiens provided the opposition and were beaten by Quebec 4–3. All of the dispensed Quebec players—Mummery, Dave Ritchie, George Carey, McDonald, Malone, Crawford, and Hall—returned to play for their old team. Paddy Moran came out of retirement to play in goal.

A real NHL game would also be played in Quebec City, the first neutral-site game in NHL history, on March 2, 1918, as the Canadiens fell 3–1 to the Ottawa Senators.

Quebec would also opt to sit out the 1918–19 NHL season, but would return for the 1919–20 campaign. Malone, Mummery, Carey, Ritchie, Marks and McDonald were all back with the club from their loan duty with other teams.

There would be few highlights during what would prove to be the lone NHL season for the franchise, despite a 4–20 campaign. One such night was January 31, 1920, when Malone scored seven goals in a win over Toronto, setting an NHL mark that's yet to be equalled.

Then on March 10, 1920, defenceman Mummery donned the pads in place of injured goalie Frank Brophy and beat the Ottawa Senators 10–4. He remains the only position player in NHL history to post a goaltending victory. Making the performance even more astonishing was the fact that the Senators would go on to win the Stanley Cup that spring.

The Quebec franchise was relocated to Hamilton on November 1, 1920, partly because the NHL felt it was a better market, but mostly to thwart former Toronto owner Eddie Livingstone's plans to put a franchise in Hamilton in the rival Canadian Hockey Association he was attempting to organize.

The Hamilton Tigers were as unsuccessful as Quebec, failing to make the playoffs in each of their first four seasons. After a surprising first-place finish in 1924–25, the Tigers were suspended and the NHL title was awarded to the Montreal Canadiens when the players went on strike over unpaid wages. Hamilton owner Percy Thompson sold the team to New York interests and they became the New York Americans for the 1925–26 season, the first NHL franchise to call the Big Apple home.

The Americans—mockingly referred to as the "Amazin' Amerks"—were equally unsuccessful on the ice. The team folded out of existence in 1942 without ever appearing in a Stanley Cup final.

TORONTO HOCKEY CLUB

The reason for the birth of the NHL, the 1917–18 Toronto club looked much like the 1916–17 Toronto NHA club, with seven of the same players. But the biggest difference was that bombastic owner Eddie Livingstone had been axed out of the picture. The pro game had struggled to make inroads with Toronto's hockey public, who often preferred the less violent amateur style of play, and it was felt this fresh start would give the team a chance to win local hockey fans over.

"Professional hockey has its chance of a lifetime to make good in Toronto this season," the *Ottawa Journal* noted. "Right now it appears as if there will be no senior OHA series this winter. Consequently, the Queen City fans will have to turn to the pro stuff for their sport.

"If the Torontos and the rest of the NHL teams deliver the goods by playing fast, clean hockey, they will earn many friends who will stick with them in the years to come.

"The new management at Toronto will also help the cause considerably."

Stepping in when Quebec couldn't ice a team, it was also felt that the presence of Ontario's most prominent city would make it easier for the NHL to be taken seriously.

"The western club will be able to place a much stronger team on the ice than Quebec could, and in addition the blue shirts will be a better attraction at home than an Ancient Capital outfit," the *Ottawa Journal* noted.

Though the team is often cited as the Toronto Arenas in modern references and in fact was owned by the Toronto Arena Company, the truth of the matter is that they weren't called the Arenas until the 1918–19 season, and were most often referred to in public as the Blues or the Blue Shirts during the 1917–18 campaign.

Hope that peace and tranquility would fall over Toronto's pro hockey team were misplaced. Jimmy Murphy was named the manager of the team, but tendered his resignation before

The Toronto Hockey Club.

a regular season game was played. It was reported at the time that Murphy had slipped on a patch of ice and was injured and unable to fulfil his duties, so Charlie Querrie stepped in to replace him as manager of the team.

The truth later surfaced that Murphy was tired of attempts by Livingstone to undermine his efforts. Querrie also briefly stepped down for similar reasons during the season, but was eventually convinced by ownership to return to the job and instructed to have Livingstone physically removed from the premises were he to show up at the rink.

On the ice, things also started off poorly. One game into the season, after using two netminders and fishing 10 pucks out of their net, Querrie made no bones about it. His team needed a netminder.

"They haven't a goaler who can stop a balloon," noted the *Ottawa Journal*.

Toronto management were considering veteran Paddy Moran, who'd been in goal as the Quebec Bulldogs won successive Stanley Cups in 1911–12 and 1912–13. The team was also taking a look at amateur Ernie Collett, who'd backstopped the Toronto Riversides to the 1915–16 OHA Senior title. But Toronto got an early Christmas present when Harry (Hap) Holmes, goalie for Toronto's 1913–14 Stanley Cup victory, as well as the 1916–17 Cup-winning Seattle Metropolitans, turned out for practice. Holmes was NHL property of the Wanderers, who sought either Ken Randall or Reg Noble in a trade for his rights, an idea that Querrie felt patently ludicrous.

When the Westmount Arena burned to the ground and the Wanderers were disbanded, Toronto grabbed Holmes in the dispersal draft. Around the same time, stalwart, stay-at-home defenceman Harry Mummery ended a contract holdout and signed with the team, further strengthening Toronto's play in its own end.

Toronto was an entertaining bunch, a group that was capable of playing spectacularly up-tempo, attacking hockey, and undoubtedly the fastest team in the league. But the Toronto club was also the hardest partying team in the NHL, and players like Reg Noble, Harry Cameron and Ken Randall enjoyed carousing away from the rink as much as they thrived on carrying the puck up ice.

Noble and Cameron were fined for what was known in the day as breaking training, but was in fact drinking to excess, staying out late and missing curfew.

Led by their captain Randall, the stormy petrel of the league, Toronto was also the toughest and dirtiest team in the NHL. The Wild West nature of the infant NHL was evident in the way Randall thumbed his nose at authority and refused to accept league discipline directed his way, declining to pay fines assessed by NHL officials until he was ultimately suspended by league president Frank Calder.

Mummery was another character, a monster of a man who tipped the scales at around 240 pounds. Yet the man they called Big Mum proved to be surprisingly fast on his skates.

A fearless shot blocker—or maybe he was just too big to get out of the way—Mummery's arrival solidified the Toronto defence. Querrie further tweaked his lineup, adding speed merchant Rusty Crawford from Ottawa and signing a gritty, fearless amateur forward named Jack Adams from the Sarnia seniors.

Noble topped Toronto with 30 goals and shared the NHL lead with 10 assists. Cameron led all NHL defencemen with 17 goals and 27 points.

Toronto won the second half title and defeated the Montreal Canadiens to win the first NHL title. Then Toronto downed the PCHA champion Vancouver Millionaires 3–2 in a five-game series to become the first NHL team to win the Stanley Cup.

The good times did not keep rolling for Toronto. The Arenas not only wouldn't get a chance to defend their title the next year, they couldn't even finish out the regular season.

Things went south quickly for the Arenas during the 1918–19 season, despite being the reigning champions. Holmes, who'd stabilized Toronto's netminding the previous season, returned to Seattle of the PCHA for the 1918–19 season, leaving the Arenas to turn to veteran Bert Lindsay... but the father of future NHLer Ted Lindsay was 38 and past his prime.

The Arenas started the 1918–19 season 1–6 and never were able to get back into the race, winning back-to-back games just twice all season. By February, spectators at Mutual Street Arena were as few and far between as Toronto victories. On February 18, 1919, prior to Toronto's 4–3 overtime loss to the Ottawa Senators, the team announced that wingers Randall and Harry Meeking had been let out of their contracts to sign with Glace Bay of the Maritime Senior League for the rest of the season, though both promised to return for the 1919–20 season. "Randall will leave a big hole in the local team," reported the *Toronto World*. This move also served to emphasize how senior hockey in Canada was more "shamateur" than amateur, when two full-fledged NHLers could immediately drop down and skate in a senior league.

A 9–2 loss February 20 at Ottawa officially eliminated the Arenas from the playoff picture. The next day, the Arenas opted to throw in the towel. The *Ottawa Journal* reported that the Arenas disbanded immediately after the loss, and that Arenas informed NHL president Frank Calder they intended to forfeit their remaining games.

"I have been notified by telephone by manager Querrie that the Arena club was through, and that their remaining two games away and at home would be defaulted," Calder announced. "I immediately got in touch with the Ottawa and Canadien clubs and suggested that the playoff series should begin at once."

With Toronto disbanded, the Canadiens and Senators met in a best-of-seven series to determine the NHL champion, Montreal emerging victorious in five games.

On November 26, 1919, Fred Hambly, chairman of the Toronto board of education, purchased the Arena Hockey Club. Many of the same hockey people, including Querrie, were involved with the new owner. After making an unsuccessful proposal to Art Duncan of the Vancouver Millionaires to sign on as player-manager, team brass brought on Harvey Sproule as the manager of the team.

Hambly also applied to the NHL to rename the team the Tecumsehs. But on December 8 he changed his mind and announced that the team would be called the St. Patricks. Frank Heffernan was signed from the amateur ranks as player-coach and given stock in the team as well.

The team operated as the St. Patricks into the 1926–27 season, winning the Stanley Cup in 1921–22, but mostly struggling to find any consistency on the ice. On February 14, 1927, it was revealed that Conn Smythe had put together a new group of investors who would purchase the franchise and rename it the Toronto Maple Leafs.

Today, the Leafs are among the NHL's most popular clubs, and certainly far and away the most popular NHL team in Canada. The Maple Leafs are second only to the Canadiens with 13 Stanley Cup triumphs. And it all started back in 1917 with the NHL's original Cup winner.

THE PLAYERS

Today, each NHL club carries a 23-player roster, of which 18 skaters and two goalies are eligible to suit up for every game. Teams play with four forward lines, three pairs of defence and two netminders, a back-up situated on the bench in case of injury or substandard play by the starter. Specific power play and penalty killing units are deployed in special teams scenarios.

In 1917, the NHL's inaugural campaign, the arena lumber bill was not nearly as extravagant because there was no need for large benches. Beyond the six players who took the ice for the start of the game, each NHL team suited up three subs, and these players who only go into action when required, generally because of an injury, a penalty, or a player tiring. It wasn't uncommon for some players to spend the entirety of a game on the ice.

The roster of NHL players for the league's first season was a who's who of hockey, including 19 future Hockey Hall of Famers. Their skill, dedication, knowledge and passion helped to shape the early game into the sport we love today. Some of their names grace the trophies doled out each year during the NHL awards night.

JACK ADAMS, CENTRE (TORONTO HOCKEY CLUB)

Toronto pursued the rugged forward for the Sarnia Sailors senior club all season before finally convincing Adams to put his name on a contract on February 9, 1918. A fast player, Adams quickly gained a reputation as someone not to be messed with, even by some of the NHL's toughest players. Montreal Canadiens defenceman Joe Hall, the NHL penalty minute leader, discovered Adams' temperament when the two tangled in the league final series. Adams boldly skated up to the veteran Hall after the latter had creased his forehead with his stick. "Take another crack at my face, you big stiff, and if we didn't have to stay out here to win the championship, you would get a healthy receipt," Adams promised his adversary.

Adams scored his first NHL goal in the championship series, helping Toronto reach the Stanley Cup, but since he was signed after the February 1 deadline he was ruled ineligible to play against the Vancouver Millionaires. Two years later, Adams would move to the west coast to play for the Millionaires, and twice led the Pacific Coast Hockey Association in penalty minutes and once in scoring.

Returning to the NHL, Adams won a second Stanley Cup with the Ottawa Senators in 1926–27 and then retired to take over as coach and general manager of the NHL's Detroit franchise. He coached the Red Wings to three Stanley Cups and won seven as a GM. Adams remains the only person to earn Stanley Cup inscriptions as a player, coach and GM.

Adams was inducted into the Hockey Hall of Fame in 1959, and the Jack Adams Award is presented annually to the NHL's coach of the year.

Stats	GP	G	A	P	PIM
1917–18	8	0	0	0	31
NHL Career	173	83	32	115	366

BILLY BELL, RIGHT WING (MONTREAL WANDERERS/ MONTREAL CANADIENS)

Though never more than a spare player during his NHL career, Bell managed to last a decade in major league hockey. He played for three NHL teams—the Montreal Wanderers, Montreal Canadiens and Ottawa Senators—and Bell scored one goal for each of those teams. He had a hard shot, but was not very accurate with it, making his name as a speedy backchecker.

Bell won a Stanley Cup with the Canadiens in 1923–24 before hanging up his blades as a player and turning to refereeing. He worked his first NHL game on January 10, 1925, and was selected to work the 1925–26 Stanley Cup final.

Stats	GP	G	A	P	PIM
1917–18	8	1	0	1	6
NHL Career	65	3	2	5	12

CLINT BENEDICT, GOALIE (OTTAWA SENATORS)

Praying Benny, as he was known due to his penchant for flopping to stop the puck, is likely responsible for the NHL's first major rule change when the league dropped the rule forbidding netminders from leaving their feet to make a save. Benedict struggled through the 1917–18 season and the Senators pondered replacing him, acquiring Sammy Hebert on loan from Toronto, though it proved to be a good thing they reconsidered.

Benedict would lead the NHL in shutouts seven times during his career, more than any netminder in league history, and he would backstop his teams to four Stanley Cup titles, three of them with Ottawa. He also led the league in wins for six straight seasons from 1918–19 through 1923–24.

Benedict posted four shutouts in leading the Montreal Maroons to the 1925–26 Stanley Cup title, and in 1930, after suffering a broken nose when struck by a Howie Morenz shot, he became the first goalie in NHL history to don a mask.

Benedict was inducted into the Hockey Hall of Fame in 1965.

Stats	GPI	GA	SO	GAA	W-L-T
1917–18	22	114	1	5.12	9-13-0
NHL Career	362	863	58	2.31	191-142-28

LOUIS BERLINQUETTE, LEFT WING (MONTREAL CANADIENS)

A speedy, clever forward who helped enhance the Canadiens' reputation as the Flying Frenchmen, Berlinquette was a veteran of pro hockey when the NHL was formed. He broke into the major-league ranks with Haileybury of the NHA in 1909, joining the Canadiens in 1912.

Playing as a spare behind the top line of Joe Malone, Didier Pitre and Newsy Lalonde, Berlinquette scored just two goals in 20 games during the 1917–18 season, but his defensive acumen made him a valuable sub. His best season in the NHL came with the Habs at the age of 34 in 1921–22, when he scored 13 goals, but the next season he lost his job to a talented rookie named Aurel Joliat and again played only sparingly.

Berlinquette's contract was sold to Saskatoon of the Western Canada Hockey League for the 1923–24 season. He returned to the NHL and spent his final two seasons with clubs in their inaugural campaign, the Montreal Maroons in 1924–25 and the Pittsburgh Pirates in 1925–26.

Stats	GP	G	A	P	PIM
1917–18	20	2	1	3	12
NHL Career	193	46	34	80	128

GEORGES (BUCK) BOUCHER, DEFENCE/CENTRE (OTTAWA SENATORS)

The oldest of four brothers who played in the NHL—his siblings Bobby, Billy and Frank would also play in the league—Georges (Buck) Boucher was a versatile player who could perform at any position on the ice other than goalie. He was a tremendous stick-handler, but his powerful strength made him important defensively. His versatility extended beyond the rink, as Boucher also excelled on the gridiron, playing fullback for the Ottawa Rough Riders, and at the baseball diamond.

Boucher won four Stanley Cups with the Senators and when his playing days ended in 1930, he turned to coaching, working behind the bench of the Senators, Montreal Maroons, St. Louis Eagles and Boston Bruins.

Boucher was enshrined in the Hockey Hall of Fame in 1960.

Stats	GP	G	A	P	PIM
1917–18	21	9	8	17	46
NHL Career	449	118	87	205	838

ART BROOKS, GOALIE (TORONTO HOCKEY CLUB)

A half-century before it became mandatory in the NHL, Brooks found himself suited up and on the bench as Toronto's back-up goalie when the NHL's inaugural season opened for the team at Montreal on December 19, 1917. Brooks spelled starter Sammy Hebert to start the second period in Toronto's 10–9 loss to the Montreal Wanderers, which made him part of league history, the first time a team had dressed and used two netminders in the same game.

Soon, Brooks' days as an NHL goalie would be history. He won his next two starts, but after a 9–2 loss to the Montreal Canadiens, Toronto acquired veteran Hap Holmes and on

January 5, 1918, handed Brooks his release. His NHL career ended with a 6.27 goals-against average.

"[Brooks] showed very little the few games he played," the *Ottawa Journal* noted. "He ducks at the high ones."

Stats	GPI	GA	SO	GAA	W-L-T
1917–18	4	23	0	6.27	2-2-0
NHL Career	4	23	0	6.27	2-2-0

MORLEY BRUCE, DEFENCE (OTTAWA SENATORS)

One of the few rookies to enter the NHL in 1917–18, the Senators had high hopes for Bruce. "Bruce should be a star in the pro ranks," the *Ottawa Journal* suggested. "He certainly is a clever stickhandler when working inside the nets but is apt to hurry after getting within scoring range. Consequently, his gunning is not as accurate as it would be if he steadied himself before firing."

Another team also had Bruce on their list and his rookie campaign ended after seven games when he was conscripted into the Canadian military. He spent the next year in military service.

Returning to action after the conclusion of the Great War, Bruce was welded to the bench as a spare, seeing little action as the Senators won the Stanley Cup in 1919–20 and 1920–21.

After leaving hockey, Bruce served as assistant secretary of the Ottawa Fire Department.

Stats	GP	G	A	P	PIM
1917–18	7	0	0	0	0
NHL Career	71	8	3	11	27

HARRY CAMERON, DEFENCE (TORONTO HOCKEY CLUB)

Harry Cameron was the closest thing to a Bobby Orr in the original NHL. He could rush the puck like a whirlwind and shoot the puck as hard as a rifle. It was claimed by netminders that Cameron could make his shot dip and curve as it approached the goal. Cameron could certainly tally at the pace of a forward, finishing the 1917–18 season with 17 goals and 27 points, a rate of more than a point a game.

Cameron set an NHL record for defencemen on December 26, 1917, that would stand until 1977, when he scored four goals in a game against the Montreal Canadiens, one of two hat tricks he counted during the season.

He added three goals and four points as Toronto won the Stanley Cup in 1917–18 and won a second Cup with the Toronto St. Patricks in 1921–22.

Cameron also played for the Canadiens and the Ottawa Senators in an NHL career that lasted through the 1922–23 season. He posted two 18-goal seasons that stood for years as the NHL single-season record for defencemen. He was inducted into the Hockey Hall of Fame in 1962.

Stats	GP	G	A	P	PIM
1917–18	21	17	10	27	28
NHL Career	128	88	51	139	189

BERT CORBEAU, DEFENCE (MONTREAL CANADIENS)

A slick stickhandler and a tough-as-nails defender, Corbeau could make things happen on the ice with his hands or his fists. Pig Iron, as he was known, Corbeau towered over most opponents, standing six feet tall, but grew weary of taking guff from smaller players. "I'm all cut up with butt-ends, slashes, kicks and wallops," Corbeau complained to the *Montreal*

Herald. "I'll say I've had enough, and plenty. I've lost a piece of a toe, I'm bruised from the neck down. I've been hooked across the throat so hard I can't swallow, and walloped on the back of the neck so it's black and blue and looks as if I had stopped washing at the ears."

Corbeau felt that he was in a no-win position, left to look like a bully if he retaliated against his smaller foes. "These birds are taking advantage of my size," Corbeau said. "It looks like a game thing for a bantam to take a crack at a big fellow, but if the big fellow hits back, the crowd will call him a big roughneck and a bum. But why should I worry about what the crowd says? The next time anybody takes a wallop at me, I'm going back at him."

Corbeau's innocent act was a tough sell with the opposition, and with good reason. Twice during his NHL career he led the league in penalty minutes. One night in Ottawa after roughing up some of the Senators, Corbeau was required to be at his elusive best when he ducked out of the way of a frozen turnip fired his way by a disgruntled fan.

Corbeau joined the Habs in 1914, winning a Stanley Cup with them in 1915–16 in the NHA. He also played in the Cup final in 1916–17 and 1918–19. Corbeau later played with the Hamilton Tigers, Toronto St. Patricks and Toronto Maple Leafs, becoming the first player to suit up for both the Canadiens and the Maple Leafs. After his playing days, he served as an NHL referee.

Corbeau's life met a tragic end on a day of celebration on September 29, 1942. Superintendent of the Midland, Ontario Foundry and Machine Company, Corbeau took 41 people out on Georgian Bay aboard his twin-engine boat to celebrate the completion of a war contract by holding a picnic at his cottage. But on the way home, the boat took on water about a mile and a half from shore. Investigations following the tragedy revealed that Corbeau need not have died, but his concern for others ultimately resulted in his own death.

"Corbeau evidently died a hero's death," reported Dr. Smirle Lawson, chief supervising coroner for Ontario. "His clothes were picked up at the shore. It seems that he reached safety himself and plunged back in again to help others." Including Corbeau, 16 people drowned that day.

Stats	GP	G	A	P	PIM
1917–18	21	8	8	16	41
NHL Career	259	63	49	112	652

JERRY COUGHLIN, RIGHT WING (TORONTO HOCKEY CLUB)

The best advice of Coughlin's career likely cost him an inscription on the Stanley Cup. While playing for Portage of the U.S. Amateur Hockey Association in 1915–16, Coughlin performed against a fellow by the name of Jack Adams, who impressed him, and he convinced Toronto manager Charlie Querrie to check out the young player. Querrie liked what he saw and eventually signed Adams. Trimming his roster to make room for the new blood, Coughlin was released.

A speedy player, Coughlin scored both of his NHL goals in Toronto's December 23, 1917 win over Ottawa. Each was tallied on a breakaway.

A true journeyman, Coughlin played just 19 NHL games between 1917–21, but managed to split those games among Toronto, Quebec, the Montreal Canadiens and Hamilton Tigers.

Stats	GP	G	A	P	PIM
1917–18	5	2	0	2	3
NHL Career	19	2	0	2	3

BILLY COUTU, DEFENCE (MONTREAL CANADIENS)

Not many can boast that they were banned from two leagues in successive seasons, but Coutu could. But we're getting ahead of ourselves.

In 1916, Coutu—he'd opted to shorten his name from Couture—signed with the Canadiens. Spelling Bert Corbeau and Joe Hall on defence, he quickly showed himself to be their equal in nefarious deeds, earning a unique handle, generally reserved for professional wrestlers and international despots: The Butcher.

"The game would no sooner start than Coutu would come plowing down from his defence post and pile into me with elbows, knees, shoulder and stick," former Ottawa Senators defenceman Georges Boucher recounted to the *Springfield Republican*.

Coutu displayed a knack with the spear and the butt end. During training camp with the Boston Bruins late in his career, Coutu carved the ear right off the side of teammate Eddie Shore's head.

"He was as awful and ungraceful a player as ever tied on a pair of skates," the *Ottawa Journal* opined. Coutu led the NHL in penalty minutes in 1920–21, won a Stanley Cup with the Canadiens in 1923–24, and captained the team in 1925–26.

Joining the Bruins the following season, after Boston lost the Stanley Cup final to Ottawa, Coutu attacked referee Jerry Laflamme outside the officials dressing room and was suspended for life from the NHL.

Canadiens owner Leo Dandurand pleaded with NHL president Frank Calder to show leniency to Coutu, noting that Coutu's wife had died in the fall and he needed to earn an income to care for his four children. Calder lifted his suspension to the extent that would allow him to play in the minor leagues. But if they thought Coutu had learned his lesson, while playing for New Haven he was suspended for the 1927–28 season from the Can-Am League after assaulting Boston Tigers player George Redding over the head with his stick.

Coutu played through most of the 1930s and after his playing days were done, shockingly became a minor pro referee.

Stats	GP	G	A	P	PIM
1917–18	20	2	2	4	49
NHL Career	244	33	21	54	478

RUSTY CRAWFORD, DEFENCE/LEFT WING (OTTAWA SENATORS/TORONTO HOCKEY CLUB)

A rancher in Prince Albert, Saskatchewan, Crawford was well-travelled on and off the ice. "He can play just as good a game on the defence as up on the line, and vice versa," the *Ottawa Journal* reported. "He is a speed artist from the word go, and it is doubtful if there is a faster skater in the league."

That speed came in handy. Because Rusty was a man on the move. Crawford played pro hockey from 1912–30, skating in six leagues and suiting up for eight teams. He was 45 when he hung up his blades.

Crawford played for five different teams in the Stanley Cup final, winning with the Quebec Bulldogs as a rookie in 1912–13 and again with Toronto in 1917–18. Toronto acquired Crawford after he was released by Ottawa, among the first midseason player transactions in NHL history. He was inducted into the Hockey Hall of Fame in 1962.

Stats	GP	G	A	P	PIM
1917–18	21	3	4	7	66
NHL Career	39	10	8	18	118

JACK DARRAGH, RIGHT WING (OTTAWA SENATORS)

Long before there was any thought of a players' union in pro hockey, Darragh was determined to fight for his rights. He was so set in his contract demands that he actually sat out the first period of Ottawa's NHL season opener, finally suiting up for the second frame after ownership acquiesced to his demands. He quit the team again in January. Suspended, Darragh agreed to return to action when the team considered coming after him for money he'd already been paid.

On the ice, Darragh was considered an unselfish player, and a determined backchecker. He was known for his slick stickhandling, clean play, deceptive speed and deadly backhand.

Darragh was a valuable spare during Ottawa's Stanley Cup dynasty of the 1920s. "He could play either wing or centre," remembered long-time NHL coach Tommy Gorman. Darragh scored back-to-back Stanley Cup-winning goals for the Senators in 1919–20 and 1920–21. He tallied 22 goals in 1919–20 and led the NHL with 15 assists in 1920–21.

Just three months after retiring from the game following the 1923–24 season, Darragh was stricken with peritonitis and died. He was 34. Darragh was enshrined in the Hockey Hall of Fame in 1962.

Stats	GP	G	A	P	PIM
1917–18	18	14	5	19	26
NHL Career	121	66	46	112	113

CORB DENNENY, CENTRE (TORONTO HOCKEY CLUB)

What he lacked in size, Corb Denneny made up for with a motor that didn't stop. The younger brother of Ottawa star Cy Denneny was a speedy backchecker and good finisher who tallied Toronto's Stanley Cup winner in 1917–18 and scored 20 goals that season, the first of his two 20-goal campaigns as an NHLer.

On January 26, 1921, Denneny scored six goals in a win over the Hamilton Tigers. Later that season, on March 7, his brother Cy would also net six goals in a win over the Tigers. They are the only siblings to score six goals in an NHL game. Corb won a second Stanley Cup with the Toronto St. Patricks in 1921–22.

He scored the final goal in the history of the St. Patricks before they were rechristened as the Maple Leafs in the midst of the 1926–27 season, but never played for the Leafs. Denneny's contract was sold to Saskatoon of the Prairie League before the team played their first game under their new name. In a pro career that lasted from 1914–31, Denneny played for 14 teams.

Stats	GP	G	A	P	PIM
1917–18	21	20	9	29	14
NHL Career	176	103	42	145	148

CY DENNENY, LEFT WINGER (OTTAWA SENATORS)

A speedster with a deadly shot, Cy Denneny retired as the NHL's greatest goal scorer. "Cy Denneny in his best form packs a hard and accurate shot," the *Ottawa Journal* noted.

Denneny scored 36 goals for the Senators in 1917–18, second only to the 44 tallied by Joe Malone of the Montreal Canadiens.

Long before Bobby Hull and Stan Mikita made it fashionable with the Chicago Blackhawks in the 1960s, Denneny was the first NHLer to play with a curve in the blade of his stick. "We didn't have those fancy machines to make our sticks just the way we wanted," Denneny explained to the *Ottawa Journal.* "I had to stand on the end of the blade and bend it. But let me tell you, putting a curve in the blade helps you control when you are shooting."

Denneny compiled a pair of 30-goal seasons and five 20-goal campaigns and when he retired from the NHL in 1929, he was the NHL's career goal-scoring leader with 248. Denneny won five Stanley Cups—four with the Senators (1919–20, 1920–21, 1922–23, 1926–27) and one with the Boston Bruins (1928–29), retiring in 1929. Denneny scored Ottawa's Stanley Cup winner in 1927 and he and his brother Corb (Toronto, 1918), along with the Richards—Henri and Maurice—are the only siblings in NHL history to score Cup winners. He later coached the Senators and worked as an NHL referee. Denneny was inducted into the Hockey Hall of Fame in 1959.

Stats	GP	G	A	P	PIM
1917–18	20	36	10	46	80
NHL Career	327	248	85	333	301

EDDIE GERARD, DEFENCE/LEFT WING (OTTAWA SENATORS)

During an era when more NHL defencemen were known for their brutality, Gerard was a gentlemanly performer who chose to play the game cleanly, never being assessed more than 20 minutes in penalties in a single season.

"He was a perfect gentleman and a wonderful athlete," former teammate Horace Merrill told the *Ottawa Journal*. "He never drank nor smoked and always kept himself in good physical condition. They do not make men any better than Eddie Gerard."

Gerard served as Ottawa's player-manager in 1917–18 and seldom left the ice, in fact playing all 77:15 of an overtime game against the Montreal Canadiens.

He won the Stanley Cup four seasons in a row beginning with Ottawa's victory in 1919–20. The Senators repeated in 1920–21 and won again in 1922–23. In between the Toronto St. Patricks won the Cup in 1921–22, but when the team ran into a rash of injuries on defence during the final series, were granted permission to borrow Gerard from the Senators.

"I could relax when the puck was on the end of Eddie's stick, knowing it would reach the other end of the rink," Ottawa goalie Clint Benedict said.

Gerard contracted a throat ailment in 1924 that brought an end to his playing days. He was named manager of the expansion

Montreal Maroons that year and in 1925–26, guided them to a Stanley Cup title. Gerard also coached the New York Americans and St. Louis Eagles in the NHL.

He never fully recovered from his illness and it claimed his life at the age of 47 on December 7, 1937. Gerard was inducted into the Hockey Hall of Fame in 1945.

Stats	GP	G	A	P	PIM
1917–18	20	13	7	20	36
NHL Career	128	50	47	97	120

JERRY GERAN, CENTRE (MONTREAL WANDERERS)

The hype surrounding the first American-trained NHLer was palpable. When Geran signed with the Montreal Wanderers on October 29, 1917, it was reported that he "comes here with the reputation of being a second Hobey Baker," comparing him to the legendary American star who was killed in the Great War.

When Geran took the ice, the evidence for such greatness was lacking. "The Wanderers tried out a new man, Geran, who played a year ago with Boston, and from what he showed he is not fast enough for professional hockey," the *Montreal Gazette* noted after Geran's NHL debut.

Geran was suitably impressed by the NHL game. "The first thing that stood out in the professional game was the resourcefulness of the players," Geran told the *Boston Herald*. "Amateur players are inclined to be too mechanical, but a pro sizes up a situation at a glance and depends on his initiative to go through."

After the Wanderers folded, Geran left the NHL and embarked upon a hockey odyssey. He won a silver medal with the United States at the 1920 Olympics, becoming the first NHLer to play in the Olympic Games. From 1921–23, Geran played in France for Club des Patineurs de Paris, becoming the first NHLer to play in a European league. Geran scored 34 goals in five games during the 1921–22 season.

Returning to the NHL in 1925–26, Geran scored five goals in 33 games for the Boston Bruins. He later went back to play in France and even tried his hand at bullfighting while in Spain.

After his European experience, Geran fancied himself as quite the continental man about town, a wine drinker when bourbon was the beverage of choice among NHL players. "They called him the Duke of Paris," Bruins owner Weston Adams Sr. remembered to the *Boston Herald*. "He wore spats and a derby. Those were his trademarks."

In 1941, Geran suggested that hockey start a players' association and stage all-star games to benefit former players who had fallen on hard times, but the idea gained little support from the moguls in the game.

Stats	GP	G	A	P	PIM
1917–18	4	0	0	0	0
NHL Career	37	5	1	6	6

JOE HALL, DEFENCE (MONTREAL CANADIENS)

Hall was a 13-season warhorse in the pro ranks when the NHL was founded, and he had an array of scar tissue—both given and received—to verify it. Bad Joe Hall, as he was known, had lost none of his abrasiveness in his later years and led the NHL with 100 penalty minutes in 1917–18.

"Hall is playing this season the best hockey he has ever shown in the east," noted Elmer Ferguson of the *Montreal Herald*. "Years may have robbed him of some of the fire which sparked forth so frequently in those old days as to earn him the title of 'Bad Man Joe' but they haven't robbed him of any of his hockey skills.

"Years of experience which ranged from one coast to the other have given him a knowledge of hockey's finer points excelled by no one, and behind this he has the physical stamina and the speed—plus the heart."

Hall turned pro in 1905 with Portage Lake of the International League, the only pro league in existence at the time. He won two Stanley Cups with the Quebec Bulldogs of the NHA, and playing for the Stanley Cup would claim Hall's life.

The Spanish influenza epidemic that raged through the world in 1918–19 claimed among its victims the 1919 Stanley Cup final between Seattle and the Canadiens. The series was cancelled when so many players fell ill that there weren't enough healthy bodies left standing to fill out lineups.

Several Montreal players were hospitalized, including Hall. He continued to go downhill and died on April 5, 1919. Hall was 37. He was enshrined in the Hockey Hall of Fame in 1961.

Stats	GP	G	A	P	PIM
1917–18	21	8	7	15	100
NHL Career	37	15	9	24	235

SAMMY HEBERT, GOALIE (TORONTO HOCKEY CLUB/ OTTAWA SENATORS)

Several NHL goaltenders have been described as having stood on their head in competition, but Sammy Hebert was the only NHL goalie who could build a piano. For more than half a century, Hebert constructed and sold pianos in Ottawa and on occasion, found time to stop some pucks.

Hebert was with the Toronto club when the 1917–18 NHL season got underway, but Toronto's goaltending was viewed as its Achilles heel at the start of the season. "He has been playing for some time now but is just fair at best," the *Ottawa Journal* suggested of Hebert.

Toronto management agreed and Hebert was replaced in early January by Hap Holmes. The Senators picked up Hebert, but he never saw any game action for Ottawa in 1917–18, though he did dress on occasion as a backup goaltender.

He played two seasons with Saskatoon of the Western Canada League and then saw two more games of NHL duty in 1923–24 with the Senators, pinch-hitting for an injured Clint Benedict.

Stats	GPI	GA	SO	GAA	W-L-T
1917–18	2	10	0	7.50	1-1-0
NHL Career	4	19	0	5.70	1-2-0

HARRY HAP HOLMES, GOALIE (TORONTO HOCKEY CLUB)

"Don't worry. Get Happy." This could have been the slogan for Toronto manager Charlie Querrie, because the season turned for his team when he turned its goaltending over to Holmes.

"Holmes can be favourably compared to [Montreal Canadiens goalie Georges] Vezina," the *Toronto World* reported, "and to our way of thinking this is the highest compliment that can be paid a netminder."

Holmes was assembling quite a resume of success as a pro, and backstopping the first NHL team to win the Stanley Cup only added to his winning ways. He'd already won Cups with the NHA's Toronto Blueshirts in 1913–14 and with the PCHA's Seattle Metropolitans in 1916–17, the latter the first American club to win the Cup. Holmes would add another Cup with the WCHL's Victoria Cougars in 1924–25, the last team from outside the NHL to win Lord Stanley's mug.

Holmes, who was follically challenged, was also known for the ball cap he wore while guarding the twine, but this accessory to his wardrobe wasn't merely a fashion statement. Like the masks that goalies don today, Hap's cap was all about protection.

Hockey rinks of that era were generally equipped with promenade seating behind the nets, balconies that extended out right to the edge of the ice surface. And these cheap seats were heavily populated with tobacco chewing and spewing marksmen.

"I swear some of those fellows used to load their tobacco with birdshot," Holmes explained to the *Windsor Star*. "After a game, my head carried so many lumps, the boys claimed I'd had an attack of chickenpox."

After his playing days, Holmes managed Cleveland's minor pro club for years and the American Hockey League named its goaltending award in his honour. Holmes was inducted into the Hockey Hall of Fame in 1972.

Stats	GPI	GA	SO	GAA	W-L-T
1917–18	16	76	0	4.73	9-7-0
NHL Career	103	264	17	2.43	39-54-10

HARRY HYLAND, RIGHT WING (MONTREAL WANDERERS/OTTAWA SENATORS)

Nearing the end of his playing days as the NHL was born, Hyland still packed a dangerous shot, was a fast skater and a tower of strength on the ice. Hyland scored five goals in his first NHL game, leading the Wanderers to their lone NHL win. In 17 games split between the Wanderers and Senators, he scored 14 goals.

"He's scrappy and game," the *Montreal Herald* noted. "More than this, he has a keen knowledge of hockey from the inside."

Hyland won a Stanley Cup with the Wanderers in 1909–10 and won the Minto Cup Canadian senior lacrosse championship with the New Westminster Salmonbellies the same season. Hyland later served as an NHL referee and was enshrined in the Hockey Hall of Fame in 1962.

Stats	GP	G	A	P	PIM
1917–18	17	14	2	16	65
NHL Career	17	14	2	16	65

EDOUARD NEWSY LALONDE, CENTRE
(MONTREAL CANADIENS)

One of his first jobs was at a newsprint plant. Friends hung the nickname Newsy on him and it stuck—much like Lalonde was known to get his stick stuck in the mid-section of unfortunate opponents who crossed his path on the ice.

"One thing about the early openings of the pro hockey season," the *Ottawa Journal* noted as the 1917–18 NHL season was about to commence, "Newsy Lalonde will have a chance to grab a few scalps as an Xmas box for himself."

Lalonde was called every name in the book as an NHLer, including patriot. Lalonde took the vast majority of his 1917–18 salary in victory bonds to aid the war effort.

The first great French Canadian superstar to play for the Canadiens, Lalonde set the tone for the fast, exciting, passionate game that the Habs would play. "Newsy is a great advertising asset to any league," Canadiens manager George Kennedy said.

Lalonde first joined the Canadiens in the NHA in 1909–10 and led that league in scoring three times. He finished as the NHL scoring leader in 1918–19 and 1920–21. Lalonde recorded a six-goal game January 10, 1920, and a five-goal game on February 16, 1921.

He played his final NHL game with the New York Americans in 1926–27 and when he retired, Lalonde's 437 goals were a pro hockey record. He coached the Americans, Canadiens and Ottawa Senators. Lalonde was inducted into the Hockey Hall of Fame in 1950.

Stats	GP	G	A	P	PIM
1917–18	14	23	7	30	51
NHL Career	99	124	42	166	151

JACK LAVIOLETTE, DEFENCE/LEFT WING
(MONTREAL CANADIENS)

Something was missing from the repertoire of the veteran Canadiens forward as the 1917–18 NHL season got underway—the famous cap that Laviolette had worn on his head through his entire career. "He's letting that $10,000 crop [of hair] blow careless-like to the breeze," the *Ottawa Journal* noted. Laviolette was reported to wear the longest hair in hockey.

Pro hockey was an old man's game in 1917–18, and among the oldest of these men was Laviolette. A pro since 1904, Laviolette was 38 and the impact of his long tour in the hockey wars was evident in his play.

"Father Time is showing his effect on Jack Laviolette, that once spectacular and popular player," the *Toronto Mail and Empire* noted. "At no stage did he display any of the pep that used to arouse enthusiasm among the spectators."

The *Ottawa Journal* begged to differ, noting that Laviolette's game began to come around as the season progressed. "Toronto critics say Jack Laviolette had lost his speed, but it hasn't got to the point where it's necessary for him to wear a tail light so that there'll be less likelihood of someone running into him while he's staggering about the ice. It takes a few weeks' activity to get the kinks out of Jack's forty-odd-year old joints—but after that, none of the youngsters can show him anything."

Among those who helped form the Canadiens in 1909, Laviolette played in two Stanley Cup finals, winning in 1915–16. His career came to an abrupt end when he lost a foot in a 1918 car accident. The Hockey Hall of Fame welcomed Laviolette into the fold in 1962.

Stats	GP	G	A	P	PIM
1917–18	18	2	1	3	6
NHL Career	18	2	1	3	6

BERT LINDSAY, GOALIE (MONTREAL WANDERERS)

The winning netminder in the first NHL game, though he enjoyed a lengthy and successful career as a puckstopper, Bert Lindsay is best known for his production. His son Ted Lindsay would enjoy a Hall of Fame career with the Detroit Red Wings and Chicago Blackhawks and is the only man in NHL history to win the Art Ross Trophy and also lead the league in penalty minutes. When Lindsay broke in with the Wings in 1944 he was the first son of an original NHLer to play in the NHL.

Bert Lindsay spent two seasons in the NHL, joining the Toronto Arenas in 1918–19 after the Wanderers folded. He twice played for the Stanley Cup, with Edmonton in 1909 and Victoria in 1914.

Following his playing days, Lindsay patented a collapsing hockey net that he felt would save players from injury, but goalies figured out they could cut down a shooter's angle by leaning on the crossbar and the novelty net never caught on.

Stats	GPI	GA	SO	GAA	W-L-T
1917–18	4	24	0	8.75	1-3-0
NHL Career	20	118	0	5.71	6-14-0

EDDIE LOWREY, CENTRE (OTTAWA SENATORS)

A spare with the Senators in 1917–18, a neck injury hampered Lowrey's season, limiting him to 12 games. He was an aggressive player, a tenacious worker, but was very weak around the nets.

Lowrey played with the Senators again in 1918–19 and with the Hamilton Tigers in 1920–21 before leaving the NHL to join the Regina Capitals of the WCHL in 1921–22. After concluding his playing days, Lowrey coached the NCAA's Michigan Wolverines from 1927–44.

Stats	GP	G	A	P	PIM
1917–18	12	2	1	3	3
NHL Career	27	2	2	4	6

JOE MALONE, CENTRE (MONTREAL CANADIENS)

The called him the Phantom, but what Malone did during the NHL's inaugural campaign continues to hold a place in the game's lore and the league's record book a century later.

After speculation that Malone would not play because he had a good job back in Quebec City and a wife and child to support, he arrived in Montreal and set the NHL on fire.

Malone scored five goals in the Canadiens season opener and just kept on scoring. He collected a trio of five-goal games, an NHL record, as is his goals-per game mark of 2.2. Malone scored 44 times in 20 games to lead the league. Malone's goal total would rule over the league until Canadiens forward Rocket Richard netted 50 in 1944–45.

"The Canadiens have augmented their sharpshooting brigade by the addition of such an able marksman as Joseph Malone," wrote Elmer Ferguson in the *Montreal Herald*.

That they did. Acquired on loan from the dormant Quebec team, when Quebec returned to active status in 1919, Malone rejoined the club and won another NHL scoring title. He netted six goals in a March 10, 1920 win over Ottawa, less than two months after Malone acquired another NHL mark that remains on the books today. On January 31, 1920, he scored an NHL-record seven goals in a win over Toronto.

Malone won three Stanley Cups—two with the Quebec Bulldogs of the NHA and one with the Canadiens in 1923–24, his farewell NHL campaign. In 1950, Malone was inducted into the Hockey Hall of Fame.

Stats	GP	G	A	P	PIM
1917–18	20	44	4	48	30
NHL Career	126	143	32	175	57

JACK MARKS, RIGHT WING (MONTREAL WANDERERS/ TORONTO HOCKEY CLUB)

Equally effective on forward or defence, in his heyday Marks was a goal scorer and a determined and responsible defensive player.

He won two Stanley Cups with the NHA's Quebec Bulldogs, but Marks, who originally turned pro in 1906, was nearing the end of the road by the time the NHL formed. He had lost much of his speed and puck carrying abilities, but was still as tenacious as ever with his backchecking, and his trademark work ethic had not abandoned him.

Marks was still Quebec property in 1917, but was loaned to the Wanderers when Quebec suspended operations and then acquired by Toronto after the Wanderers folded.

After sitting out the 1918–19 season, Marks returned to action when Quebec joined the NHL, but packed it in for good after playing one game.

Stats	GP	G	A	P	PIM
1917–18	6	0	0	0	0
NHL Career	7	0	0	0	4

JACK MCDONALD, LEFT WING (MONTREAL WANDERERS/MONTREAL CANADIENS)

A speedy forward with excellent playmaking skills, McDonald was a Stanley Cup winner with Quebec of the NHA in

1911–12. McDonald was a well-travelled player, seeing action with four NHL teams—Wanderers, Canadiens, Quebec and Toronto—in five seasons.

In November 1920, McDonald was involved in one of the largest trades in the early years of the NHL when the Hamilton Tigers dealt his NHL rights along with Harry Mummery and Dave Ritchie to the Canadiens for Jerry Coughlin and the season-loan of Billy Coutu.

McDonald played for the Canadiens in the ill-fated 1919 Stanley Cup, scoring the first Stanley Cup overtime goal ever netted by an NHL player. He saw three separate tours of duty with the Habs—from 1918–19, 1920–21 and 1921–22.

Stats	GP	G	A	P	PIM
1917–18	12	12	2	14	15
NHL Career	68	26	14	40	30

HARRY MEEKING, LEFT WING (TORONTO HOCKEY CLUB)

Meeking won Stanley Cups with the first NHL team (Toronto) and the last team to win the trophy from outside the NHL (WCHL Victoria Cougars, 1924–25). He scored three goals in Toronto's 7–3 playoff victory over the Montreal Canadiens on March 11, 1918, becoming the first NHL player to net a hat trick in a post-season game.

"He checks like a fiend and his work around the net is good," the *Toronto World* noted. "Meeking has speed and stickhandling ability but he evinced a desire to mix it up with his opponents," added the *Ottawa Journal*.

Moving west to play for the Victoria Aristocrats of the PCHA in 1919, Meeking excelled as a rover in the seven-man game still employed out west. He led the PCHA with 57 penalty minutes in 1920–21 and scored 13 goals in 1921–22.

He would return to the NHL in 1926–27 as an original member of the expansion Detroit Cougars, today's Red Wings. He was traded to the Boston Bruins during that season and finished his NHL days there, playing his farewell NHL games in the Stanley Cup final that spring as the Bruins were vanquished by the Ottawa Senators.

Stats	GP	G	A	P	PIM
1917–18	21	10	9	19	28
NHL Career	65	18	13	31	66

HORACE MERRILL, DEFENCE (OTTAWA SENATORS)

A long-time member of the Senators during their NHA days, Merrill began the season on the retired list, but the veteran was lured back to the ice and signed with Ottawa in February.

A steady, stay-at-home type, Merrill was neither speedy nor graceful on skates. There was nothing flashy about him, but Merrill was a strong defender who knew how to shoot the attacking forwards into the corner. Despite his powerful strength, Merrill seldom played the game beyond the rules and gained a reputation as a hard but clean player. He served as club captain with the Senators in 1916–17.

A champion paddler, Merrill won Canadian titles in canoeing at the half mile and one-mile distances. He was the Canadian senior champion in the men's single canoe from 1907–1909.

Stats	GP	G	A	P	PIM
1917–18	3	0	0	0	3
NHL Career	8	0	0	0	3

HARRY MUMMERY, DEFENCE (TORONTO HOCKEY CLUB)

Big Mum was the human freight car. Standing 5–11 and weighing between 220–240 pounds, Mummery was a frightening sight on blades, and opponents generally cut him a wide swath.

It was said that if Mummery fell, the arena windows rattled. The joke was that if he sprawled on top of the puck, it would be flatter than a wafer.

In the off-season, Mummery was a locomotive engineer for CP Rail and his work often prevented him from getting on the ice at the start of the season.

A tremendous shot blocker, Mummery was thorough in his checking, mobile for his size and a good puck mover. He scored 15 goals with the Montreal Canadiens in 1920–21.

"He was so big he was frightening at times," Ottawa Senators star Cy Denneny recalled to the *Ottawa Journal*. "There were times when he'd start down the ice and start swaying on one foot or the other, and one of a wingman's worries was that he'd lose his balance and topple on you. You had to watch yourself in between the boards and Mummery."

To help protect his girth, Mummery utilized a rubber band that was 12 feet long and 18 inches wide. Prior to suiting up in his gear, Mummery would hold one end of the rubber band while the trainer held the other and he'd twirl like a top until his belly was encased inside his impromptu girdle.

Born in Chicago but raised in Brandon, Manitoba, Mummery won Stanley Cups with Toronto in 1917–18 and Quebec in 1912–13. He donned the pads and tended goal in four NHL games, posting two victories.

Mummery's eating habits were legendary. He was once, mere minutes before game time, found by Toronto teammate Jack Adams cooking a steak on the business end of a shovel over the open flame of the Mutual Street Arena boiler. His savage appetite also ended his NHL career with the Hamilton Tigers in 1922–23. Mummery joined Saskatoon of the Western Canada League. Unable to find hockey pants that would fit over his bulk, the Saskatoon club com-missioned a tent company to make him a special pair.

As a prank, Mummery's teammates painted a smiley face on the seat of Mummery's pants. He took the ice wearing his happy pants, and was an immediate crowd favourite.

Stats	GP	G	A	P	PIM
1917–18	18	3	3	6	41
NHL Career	107	33	19	52	23

FRANK NIGHBOR, CENTRE (OTTAWA SENATORS)

Considered the key cog in Ottawa's hockey machine, Nighbor scored an NHA-leading 41 goals for the Senators in 1916–17, but he was enlisted as a mechanic in the Royal Flying Corps and sta-tioned in Toronto, so where—if at all—he would play in 1917–18 remained up in the air as the NHL season got underway.

Ottawa was seeking to sign him, while Toronto was working to broker a deal with the Senators for his rights. The Senators finally signed Nighbor two games into the season, but he didn't take a regular turn with them until the second half of the season after gaining leave from the RFC.

The Pembroke Percolator, as he was known, was also a bril-liant defensive player and master of the poke check. Ottawa's checking system revolved around the wingers forcing the puck carrier into the middle of the ice, where with a deft sweep of his stick, Nighbor would separate the player from the puck. "You really didn't have to have a defence out there in front of a goalminder so long as you had Frank Nighbor at centre," Ottawa goalie Clint Benedict once remarked to the *Ottawa Journal.*

One of the classiest players to suit up in the NHL, Nighbor was the first winner of both the Hart and Lady Byng Trophies. He twice led the NHL in assists and won five Stanley

Cups—four with the Senators and one with the PCHA's Vancouver Millionaires.

Nighbor concluded his NHL playing days with the Toronto Maple Leafs in 1929–30. The Hockey Hall of Fame welcomed Nighbor in 1947.

Stats	GP	G	A	P	PIM
1917–18	10	11	8	19	6
NHL Career	349	139	98	237	249

REG NOBLE, CENTRE (TORONTO HOCKEY CLUB)

Noble could best be described as the last of the first. When he played his final games with the Montreal Maroons in 1932–33 Stanley Cup play-offs, Noble was the last original NHL player to be active in the league.

He left the game as a rock-solid stay-at-home defender, a far cry from the swashbuckling Noble who played for the Toronto club in 1917–18. Noble was big and fast, a fine stickhandler who was also a hard checker, good finisher and playmaker, and his brain matter was filled with solid hockey sense.

Noble led Toronto's Stanley Cup winners in 1917–18 with 30 goals and his 10 assists were an NHL high. He won another Cup with the Toronto St. Patricks in 1921–22, but when he joined the expansion Montreal Maroons in 1924–25, most felt the game had passed Noble by.

Not Maroons manager Eddie Gerard. He moved Noble back to defence, a position at which he excelled. In 1925–26 Noble added a third Stanley Cup with the Maroons while patrolling the blue line for Montreal.

Detroit manager Jack Adams, Noble's teammate on that 1917–18 Toronto Stanley Cup team, also saw Noble as a veteran presence who could stabilize his rebuilding team. Arriving in Detroit in 1927–28, Noble helped to shepherd his new team into the playoffs for the first time in franchise history in

1928–29. Later an NHL referee, Noble was inducted into the Hockey Hall of Fame in 1962.

Stats	GP	G	A	P	PIM
1917–18	20	30	10	40	35
NHL Career	510	168	106	274	916

GEORGE O'GRADY, DEFENCE (MONTREAL WANDERERS)

A star some years earlier with the Garnets of the Montreal Senior League, O'Grady sought to make a comeback with the Wanderers. But as was the case in his previous stints with the Wanderers in the old NHA, O'Grady's game simply wasn't up to snuff at hockey's highest level.

Though an amateur star, he didn't have the necessary speed for the NHL game. When the Wanderers folded, there were no other takers for O'Grady's services in the NHL or PCHA and he simply disappeared from the hockey scene.

Stats	GP	G	A	P	PIM
1917–18	4	0	0	0	0
NHL Career	4	0	0	0	0

EVARISTE PAYER, CENTRE (MONTREAL CANADIENS)

Freshly returned from military service in the Great War, Payer answered the call of his old squad when injuries and incarceration threatened to shorten the Canadiens' bench.

Payer played for the Habs in the NHA from 1910–12 prior to enlisting in the Canadian Forces and heading off to fight in Europe. Payer spent three years in military service between 1914–17 and was just recently returned to Canada when the Canadiens, without Newsy Lalonde (lacerated foot) and wondering whether they'd have Joe Hall, who'd been arrested for an on-ice assault in Toronto, looked to be shy of bodies.

Payer stepped forward to help his short-staffed club when they played in Ottawa, not far from his home in Gatineau, Quebec, the only NHL game for which he suited up, his last taste of pro hockey.

Stats	GP	G	A	P	PIM
1917–18	1	0	0	0	0
NHL Career	1	0	0	0	0

DIDIER PITRE, RIGHT WING (MONTREAL CANADIENS)

A pro since 1904, the ravages of time did nothing to slow down Pitre, known as the bullet of the east and the human cannonball for his blazing speed. "Despite the fact that many winters, summers and other seasons have trespassed upon his frame, he can still give cards and spades to the youngsters in sheer dizzy speed," the *Montreal Herald* noted. "There isn't a player in all the east who can stride out with this portly old veteran."

Pitre was equally as fast skating backwards or forwards and his shot was terrific. Ottawa goalie Clint Benedict classified it as the most dangerous in the NHL. His determination and work ethic were also laudable. "Pitre earns every cent he gets," Canadiens manager George Kennedy told the *Winnipeg Tribune*. "He would play until he dropped of sheer exhaustion. I consider him one of the greatest athletes in the country."

Pitre's sense of humour was also legendary. Checked hard into the boards during a game, a female fan leaned out over the prone Pitre and hollered, "Ruffian" in his direction. Pitre looked up, smiled and said, "Thank you lady," before regaining his footing and ambling back into the action.

The first player ever signed by the Canadiens in 1910, Pitre played 13 seasons with the Habs and skated in four Stanley Cup finals, winning with Montreal in 1915–16. His last NHL season was 1922–23. Pitre was enshrined in the Hockey Hall of Fame in 1962.

Stats	GP	G	A	P	PIM
1917–18	20	17	6	23	29
NHL Career	128	64	33	97	87

KEN RANDALL, DEFENCE/RIGHT WING (TORONTO HOCKEY CLUB)

A strong defensive presence, Randall was also a player who regularly crossed the line of the rulebook and paid a price for his actions. The *Ottawa Journal* described Randall as "a detriment to the game.

"Randall, the Toronto captain is another one of those players who thinks that his sole object on the ice is to get an opponent, no matter how he does it."

He finished second in the NHL in 1917–18 with 96 penalty minutes, and Randall was also piling up fines. But in the wild west landscape of the early NHL, he flatly refused to pay his debt to the league and continued to play.

Finally, prior to a game against Ottawa, NHL President Frank Calder informed the Toronto club that until Randall made good on his overdue payments—which had accumulated to $35 by that point—he could not play, becoming the first player to be suspended in NHL history.

Randall turned pro with Port Hope in 1909 and made a failed bid for the Stanley Cup with the Ontario club and with Sydney, Nova Scotia before winning the trophy with Toronto in 1917–18 and again in 1921–22. Randall could play up on the wing or back on the defence.

He also played for the Hamilton Tigers and New York Americans in an NHL career that lasted until 1926–27.

Stats	GP	G	A	P	PIM
1917–18	19	12	2	14	96
NHL Career	217	69	35	104	503

DAVE RITCHIE, DEFENCE (MONTREAL WANDERERS/ OTTAWA SENATORS)

Zipping down the Westmount Arena ice the night of December 19, 1917 and depositing the puck behind Toronto goalie Sammy Hebert one minute after the opening faceoff, Montreal Wanderers defenceman Dave Ritchie etched his name forever in the history books as the scorer of the first goal in NHL history. But he wasn't done: less than a minute later, Ritchie fed Jack McDonald for a goal, earning the first assist in league history.

Ritchie was the original Eric Lindros, only in reverse. It was Lindros who, in 1991, when made the first selection of the NHL entry draft by the Quebec Nordiques, refused to play in Quebec.

Ritchie, though, only wanted to play in Quebec. When the Bulldogs ceased operations for the 1917–18 season, the Ottawa Senators planned to nab Ritchie in the Quebec dispersal draft, but Ritchie insisted he'd prefer to play for one of the Montreal teams.

His reasoning was more personal than professional. Ritchie held down a job in a munitions plant in Three Rivers, Quebec. Ottawa heeded Ritchie's wishes, allowing him to go to the Wanderers and claiming Rusty Crawford instead.

Three years earlier, Wanderers manager Dickie Boon had scouted Ritchie as an amateur and sought to turn him pro, but lost out in a bidding war to Quebec.

As it turned out, when the Wanderers folded, Ritchie ended up finishing out the 1917–18 season with the Senators, making it to as many games as his work commitments would permit. Speedy and skilled, an excellent puck carrier and stickhandler, Ritchie's only weakness was his defensive play.

"I wish I had been fortunate enough to land him," Canadiens manager George Kennedy said.

He continued his vagabond existence, playing for the Toronto Arenas in 1918–19, Quebec in 1919–20 and with Kennedy's Canadiens in 1920–21.

Four years later, Ritchie would make a comeback with the Canadiens, playing five late-season games in 1924–25. He'd be lured out of retirement again in 1925–26, suiting up for another pair of games with the Habs.

By January 30 of the 1925–26 NHL season, Ritchie was wearing another uniform. He was added to the league's refereeing staff and made his debut with a whistle handling a Montreal Maroons-Boston Bruins game at the Montreal Forum.

His debut was a successful one, albeit for one misstep. As he and fellow official Cooper Smeaton headed back to the ice for the second period, they locked the dressing room door behind them, unwittingly trapping NHL President Frank Calder in the room. Calder was eventually freed from his prison midway through the frame when someone finally became aware of his pounding on the door.

Stats	GP	G	A	P	PIM
1917–18	17	9	8	17	21
NHL Career	57	15	11	26	48

ART ROSS, DEFENCE (MONTREAL WANDERERS)

Though he was no longer the same hockey great that he'd been in his younger days, Ross was part of the NHL from its birth in 1917 as player-manager of the Wanderers. As a player, he accepted his role as a spare, understanding his physical limitations, but his hockey mind was just as astute as ever. He'd lost a step but made up for it with his savvy on the ice.

"Ross stands out as the brainiest, most consistently brilliant player over a long period of years, that the game has ever known," the *Ottawa Journal* suggested. "Six feet in height, perfectly proportioned, always in the pink of condition, Ross in his heyday added to those assets terrific speed and a stick wizardry that was little short of marvelous."

Even in charge of the weak Wanderers, Ross still strived every day to make them a better club. "Ross never gives up hope," the *Ottawa Journal* reported. "It was that never-say-die spirit that made him a great hockey player."

The man for whom the NHL scoring championship trophy is named scored but one NHL goal that first season. But Ross made an impact on the game in so many ways. He improved the design of the puck so it slid better on the ice and redesigned the net so that pucks didn't bound out as easily.

After the Wanderers folded, Ross refereed in the NHL and coached the Hamilton Tigers, but his true claim to NHL fame came when he was named coach and GM of the expansion Boston Bruins in 1924, the NHL's first U.S.-based team. He coached the Bruins for 17 seasons and served as GM until 1954, adding three more Stanley Cup titles to his resume. Ross was inducted into the Hockey Hall of Fame in 1945.

Stats	GP	G	A	P	PIM
1917–18	3	1	0	1	12
NHL Career	3	1	0	1	12

HAMBY SHORE, DEFENCE (OTTAWA SENATORS)

A husky chap who was large for his day at six feet tall and 175 pounds, Shore possessed the skill to play the rover position in the days of seven-man hockey, but was most comfortable on defence. He joined the Ottawa club in 1904 at the age of 18 and skated alongside some of the legendary Silver Seven, including Billy Gilmour, Frank McGee and Harvey Pulford, seeing action in the famous 1905 Stanley Cup series between Ottawa and the team from Dawson City, Yukon, the first of five times that Shore would play in a Stanley Cup final.

Due to his size and speed, the young Shore was often deployed to shadow the opposition's best player and was adept at frustrating the top performers with his tenacious checking. He was moved back to defence in 1909 when Cyclone Taylor left Ottawa to join the Renfrew club.

If there was a weakness in Shore's game, it was a lack of self confidence. That malady seemed to entangle him in its grasp during the 1917–18 NHL season and Shore was released by the Senators right before the end of season.

He would never play hockey again. Shore was ailing with a cold during much of the 1917–18 NHL season, and in the fall it would develop into a bout of Spanish Influenza. Shore was one of the many victims of this worldwide epidemic when the ailment claimed his life on October 13, 1918 at the age of 32. A benefit game was held on March 1, 1919 between the Senators and an all-star aggregate of Ottawa amateurs to raise funds to purchase a monument for Shore's gravesite.

Stats	GP	G	A	P	PIM
1917–18	20	3	8	11	51
NHL Career	20	3	8	11	51

RAYMIE SKILTON, DEFENCE (MONTREAL WANDERERS)

The Great War brought Skilton to Montreal, but it was his skill on skates that brought Skilton to the NHL. A munitions expert, Skilton was sent to Canada to help modernize the Canadian war plants after the United States entered the war in 1917.

A star amateur player from Boston, Skilton made his NHL debut for the Wanderers on December 22, 1917, following Jerry Geran as the second U.S.-born and trained player in league history. But his was a short-lived career.

Skilton was bedridden with flu shortly after his one-game stint and by the time he'd recovered, the Wanderers franchise had folded.

He returned to Boston and to the amateur ranks later in the season, though that didn't sit well with some who felt Skilton was now a pro. But he insisted this wasn't the case at all and was backed up in his testimony by Geran.

"I played in that game with Skilton and know that he did not receive a penny for playing and, moreover, there is no record at the National Hockey [League] headquarters that he ever signed a contract," Geran told the *Boston Herald*. "Skilton played that one game for the pure love of hockey and nothing more."

Stats	GP	G	A	P	PIM
1917–18	1	0	0	0	0
NHL Career	1	0	0	0	0

ALF SKINNER, RIGHT WING (TORONTO HOCKEY CLUB)

When looking for keys to Toronto's 1917–18 Stanley Cup triumph, you should start with Alf Skinner. He scored eight goals in the five-game Cup final series with the Vancouver Millionaires, including the first hat trick ever tallied by a NHL player in a Stanley Cup game, after netting just 13 goals in 20 regular-season games.

An aggressive forward, sometimes Skinner crossed the line between the rules of the game and the rules of the street. He had ability and he had courage. Skinner was a fast skater, but an erratic performer who was not known for his dedication to fitness. He was a splendid stickhandler equipped with a wicked if wild shot.

Skinner certainly turned the head of Vancouver manager Frank Patrick, and when the Toronto club folded up shop during the 1918–19 NHL season he swooped in and signed Skinner to a PCHA contract. Skinner spent the next four seasons with Vancouver, potting 20 goals in 1920–21 and playing in four Stanley Cup final series.

Returning to the NHL for the 1924–25 campaign, Skinner began an odyssey that would see him suit up for three first-year expansion teams over the final two seasons of his big-league career. He began with the Montreal Maroons in 1924–25 and was traded that season to the Boston Bruins. The following season, Skinner joined the Pittsburgh Pirates. But his best days were behind him. Playing 34 games during that span, he tallied a solitary goal.

Stats	GP	G	A	P	PIM
1917–18	20	13	5	18	34
NHL Career	70	26	11	37	90

PHIL STEVENS, CENTRE/DEFENCE (MONTREAL WANDERERS)

A four-year veteran with the Wanderers, Stevens was one of the few players on the club's NHL roster who showed any significant major-league experience. He began his career as a forward but spent most of the 1917–18 campaign in the Wanderers' top defensive pairing alongside Dave Ritchie.

When the Wanderers folded, Stevens entered military service and was out of hockey until the 1921–22 season, when he joined the Montreal Canadiens. He spent one season with the Habs, and then headed west to play for Saskatoon of the Western Canada League. After three seasons with the Sheiks, he got into a contract squabble and opted to hold out, working in the automobile business in Springfield, Massachusetts. The Boston Bruins were short a defenceman and reached out to Stevens, successfully getting his name on a contract. Stevens played his final 17 NHL games with the Bruins in 1925–26.

Returning to play for Saskatoon of the minor pro Prairie League, Stevens suffered a broken nose but made pro hockey history on February 28, 1927, wearing a wire cage to protect his injured nose, becoming the first player to ever don facial protection in a pro game. When the Prairie League folded in 1928, Stevens headed farther west, signing on as captain and player/coach of the California Hockey League's Oakland Sheiks.

Stats	GP	G	A	P	PIM
1917–18	4	1	0	1	3
NHL Career	25	1	0	1	3

KEN THOMPSON, LEFT WING (MONTREAL WANDERERS)

A star performer in the Montreal City League, Thompson made his pro debut with the Wanderers on December 27, 1916, starting on right wing in a 5–2 NHA loss against the Quebec Bulldogs.

"Kenny Thompson, Tetreault and James Roy, City League players, were tried out by Wanderers and they tried hard," the *Montreal Gazette* reported of Thompson's pro debut.

The Wanderers held high hopes for Thompson, who'd led the Montreal Manufacturers League in scoring in 1914–15. But things didn't pan out. Thompson saw limited ice time and scored just one goal in 14 games and it came in a 17–6 late-season loss to Quebec, though he did impress on that night.

"Thompson, a recruit from the Montreal City League, showed about the best form for the visitors," the *Montreal Gazette* noted. "He checked back hard, and was continually rushing." Thompson played his lone NHL game on December 26, 1917, a 6–3 loss to the Ottawa Senators.

Stats	GP	G	A	P	PIM
1917–18	1	0	0	0	0
NHL Career	1	0	0	0	0

GEORGES VEZINA, GOALIE (MONTREAL CANADIENS)

The man in whose memory the NHL named the trophy it presents annually to the most valuable goaltender was certainly worthy of such recognition. Cool and almost statuesque in his work, Vezina was of high ability.

"Georges stands up there like [baseball player] Nap Lajoie and clouts them off with his big stick, or does a soccer turn and boots them with his toes," the *Montreal Herald* noted.

Canadiens trainer Ernie Cook echoed this description of Vezina's puck-stopping talents. "Vezina was a man with uncanny skill in kicking the puck away from the net," Cook recalled to the *Boston Herald-American*. His moral character was of equal calibre.

"If there was any argument about a goal around his net, then ask Georges," NHL referee Cooper Smeaton informed the *Ottawa Citizen*. "If it was a goal, Georges would say, 'Yes.' If it was not a goal, he would say, 'No.' Whatever he said, you knew that it was straight."

He backstopped the Canadiens to a pair of Stanley Cup titles and posted the first shutout in Stanley Cup history. Vezina recorded a 1.97 goals-against average in 1923–24, the first NHL goalie to go under two for an entire season.

Vezina joined the Canadiens for the 1910–11 NHA season and played every game in the Habs net—355 in a row—until the night of November 28, 1925, as Montreal played host to the Pittsburgh Pirates. Gaunt and haggard and running a temperature, Vezina insisted on taking his usual place between the posts.

Near the end of the first period, Vezina collapsed in front of his net and lapsed into unconsciousness. He was carried from the ice by teammates, never to return.

A few days later, it was revealed that the legendary Montreal goaler was afflicted with tuberculosis. Vezina's health deteriorated quickly. He lost 35 pounds in a couple of weeks. He died on March 27, 1926. A moment of silence in his memory was held the following night as the Ottawa Senators and Montreal Maroons battled for the NHL title.

"I doubt if hockey will ever know his like again," Canadiens manager Leo Dandurand told the *Canadian Press*. The NHL began presenting the Vezina Trophy in 1926–27 and Vezina was named to the Hockey Hall of Fame in 1945.

Stats	GPI	GA	SO	GAA	W-L-T
1917–18	21	84	1	4.93	12-9-0
NHL Career	190	633	13	3.27	103-81-5

THE NHL
IN ITS INFANCY

As the NHL prepared for its inaugural season, there was a lot of optimism that the end of the infighting among the league's ownership group and the downsizing of the loop could make for some spectacular hockey.

"The slicing down to a four-club affair of the Eastern pro hockey is going to be the means of giving hockey fans one of the best races in the history of the game in these parts," the *Ottawa Journal* opined. "When the NHL season opens on December 19, all four teams, Ottawa, Canadiens, Wanderers and Toronto, will go into the race all having a chance to cop. The team that wins out will deserve the honour."

The league unveiled its schedule on December 3, 1917, proposing a 24-game campaign for each team, divided into two halves, with the winners of each half clashing in a home-and-home total goals playoff series for the NHL title.

The owners of Montreal's Jubilee Rink even offered to put forth a trophy for the championship of the NHL if the Canadiens and Wanderers would agree to play all of their games at the Jubilee Rink during the coming season. Though that didn't happen initially, circumstances would unfold early in the season that would make the Jubilee Rink home to the Canadiens by default.

NHL President Frank Calder announced that to cut down on travel during wartime, hometown referees would work all regular season NHL games. But he instructed arena managers that officials required their own dressing room and it would be forbidden for anyone other than referees to enter that room.

It was jokingly suggested that, unlike the players, referees would not be in short supply. "President-elect Frank Calder needn't worry about some of his hockey referees," the *Ottawa Journal* scoffed. "Blind men are exempt from the draft, anyway."

Calder announced that each team would pay an undisclosed levy directly to the Red Cross out of every game's gate receipts in order to support the war effort, though cynics felt that this was just a ploy to ensure that the government didn't rule hockey an unnecessary venture during wartime. Some argued hockey was using up scant resources, and that the government should ban the sport for the duration of the war. Similar discussions were underway south of the border regarding Major League Baseball. In an effort to come across as more patriotic, the Chicago Cubs hired a band to perform the Star-Spangled Banner during the 1918 World Series against the Boston Red Sox, the forerunner to today's scenario where national anthems are played prior to every sporting event.

Among the NHL's first orders of business was to allocate the players from the dormant Quebec team. On November 26, 1917, the Montreal Canadiens received Joe Hall, Walter Mummery, and Joe Malone, the Montreal Wanderers selected George Carey, Jack McDonald, Jack Marks, and Dave Ritchie, the Ottawa Senators claimed Russell (Rusty) Crawford and the Toronto Arenas grabbed Skull Johnson and Harry Mummery.

JOE MALONE

All of the moves were understood to be loans from the Bulldogs, and the players would revert back to Quebec if and when the Bulldogs' franchise revived. Just when it seemed like pro hockey's problems were behind them, more dilemmas came to the fore. Montreal Wanderers manager Art Ross threatened to drop out of the fledgling NHL if the other league teams did not contribute additional players to his franchise.

"Unless the other clubs hand us over players at once, the Wanderers will not think of operating this season," Ross said.

Three of the players awarded to the Wanderers from the dormant Quebec franchise—forwards Carey and McDonald and defenceman Ritchie—refused to report to Montreal. Sprague Cleghorn was done for the season due to a broken ankle and his brother Odie Cleghorn, declared unfit for military service by the draft board, was unlikely to be granted permission to play hockey.

"How can we make any decent showing?" Ross asked. "We have lots of amateur material out with us but this will not make us strong enough to cope with the other teams.

"It is far better to suspend all together."

The Wanderers demanded that the Montreal Canadiens hand over forward Malone and defenceman Hall, forward/defenceman Crawford be given to them by Ottawa and Johnson and Harry Mummery be turned over by Toronto in order for them to be able to ice a competitive club. Ross pointed out that the other teams were well-stocked with major league material, while his bench was relatively short of top-level talent.

"Now look at the other clubs," Ross said. "Canadiens, who won the championship last season, are practically complete again, and they secure Joe Malone, Joe Hall and Walter Mummery. Ottawa, who were runners-up last season, asked for only Crawford of the Quebec players and they secured him. Toronto have practically their full team of last season before they suspended and now they secure Johnson and Harry Mummery."

Ross's plea was met largely with indifference from the other NHL clubs. Some felt that the complaint was more a case of Wanderers owner Sam Lichtenhein crying wolf.

"Let Wanderers get out," Canadiens owner/manager George Kennedy told the *Ottawa Journal*. "Who cares? So far as I am concerned, the sooner Wanderers quit, the better.

"I have friends in Quebec who would be glad to jump in right now and furnish a good team in Wanderers' place."

Ottawa secretary Martin Rosenthal, while not as blunt as Kennedy, also saw the Wanderers complaints as being ill-timed.

"We are not making players for other cities," Rosenthal told the *Ottawa Citizen*. "When the allotment of players was made at Montreal at the meeting of the National Hockey League, we asked for only one player, and no objection was raised when we drew Crawford.

"It was agreed upon that whoever won the toss between the Wanderer and Canadien delegates should get the choice of McDonald or Malone."

Calder insisted all this talk was news to him, and that the Wanderers had not contacted him with concerns regarding their ability to ice a team.

"I have not received any official notification from the Wanderers," Calder said. "At the same time I do not believe the rumours that have come to my ears."

Calder was waiting to confer with Lichtenhein upon his return to Montreal from a New York business trip.

"The president and owner of the Wanderers is not a quitter," Calder said. "In all the years I have been associated with him in sport, I've never before heard him talk quit. On the contrary, he was the gamest attacker we had."

It was pointed out to Ross that he was a bit late to scream about a player shortage.

"The time to complain about a scarcity of players was before the schedule was made up," Kennedy said. "Not now."

However sympathetic Calder was to Ross's plight, he was forced to agree with Kennedy about this.

"I doubt if the other teams will care to be held up at the last minute when all the arrangements for the season have been made," Calder said.

While some of the other team owners compared Ross to the Bolshevik revolutionaries who were at this time overthrowing the Czar in Russia, he received 100 percent support from Wanderers owner Lichtenhein.

Frank Calder.

"You may say it for me and make it as emphatic as you can, that unless the Wanderers get some players from some of the other clubs of the National Hockey League, the Red Bands will not have a team this season," Lichtenhein said when contacted in New York where he was attending the annual meetings of baseball's International League.

Lichtenhein also owned the minor pro Montreal Royals baseball team, but it was hockey that was nonetheless occupying his mind and his time.

"Unless I have favorable replies from the other clubs by the time I arrive home, I will immediately withdraw from the pro league," Lichtenhein said. "Under existing conditions, I don't care whether the Wanderers play or not."

Kennedy demanded that the league fine Ross for threatening to pull the Wanderers out of the NHL, which Ross found quite funny.

"I think his head needs some attention from a competent source," Ross said of Kennedy.

The problem was ultimately resolved when it was agreed that both Mummery boys, Harry and Walter, would be handed over to the Wanderers, along with forward Tommy Smith, a former Canadiens player.

Out west, changes were also afoot. On December 20, 1917, Pacific Coast Hockey Association president Frank Patrick officially announced that, due to a shortage of available players, Spokane would be dropped from the league and that Vancouver, Seattle and Portland would comprise a three-team outfit for the 1917–18 season, with regular-season play commencing on December 28. Each of the three teams would play 18 games.

This reduction in teams and all-out pursuit of personnel served to emphasize exactly how the war had thinned out hockey's talent pool. With so many great players overseas, the battle for what players were left grew more intense with each passing day.

Unhappy with goaltending of Sammy Hebert and Art Brooks, Toronto sought to get veteran Paddy Moran, but Moran wasn't about to leave a good job in Quebec for the uncertainty of pro hockey. There was also speculation that Toronto intended to make a strong bid for Wilfrid Box, the star of the Toronto Dentals Allan Cup championship team, but this was quickly shot down as nothing more than a publicity stunt.

"The press agent idea that interest in professional hockey is enhanced by the publication of mysterious hints that some 'crack amateur' is about to strengthen the pro game by abandoning his amateur status, 99 times out of 100 of these tales can be set down

Charlie Querrie.

as deliberate fakes," the *Toronto Globe* claimed. "Concerning the latest of them, Bill Box of Toronto Dentals says that he not only never considered such a thing, but he never was approached."

Likewise, Toronto manager Charlie Querrie was dumbfounded at reports that he was negotiating with amateur Luke Imbleau of Renfrew, Ontario. "If Imbleau is coming, someone else is buying players for me," Querrie told the *Toronto Star*.

With all of this shuffling, juggling and skullduggery finally settled, it was time to put this show on ice.

As the NHL season got underway, the Montreal Canadiens were viewed as the team to beat, and with good reason. The Stanley Cup champions in 1915–16, the Habs had also won the NHA title in 1916–17 before falling in the Cup final to the Seattle Metropolitans.

With almost their entire team intact, the Canadiens picked up 41-goal shooter Malone and tough-as-nails defenceman Hall in the dispersal draft of the players from the dormant Quebec franchise. They were loaded for bear and were the No. 1 draw on the NHL circuit.

"The boys are playing very harmoniously together but the thing that pleased me and astonished me the most was the tremendous crowd that came to see us," Kennedy said in the *Ottawa Journal* after an early season win over the Senators. There were 6,000 in attendance the first time the Habs visited Ottawa, compared to the scant gathering of 3,500 that turned up to view the first visit of the Wanderers.

"Ontario may not like the Canadiens in other ways, but they certainly are ready to pay money to see them play hockey," Kennedy said.

The operators of the Toronto Hockey Club felt they had the makings of a winner and figured that if they could work out a deal to bring centre Frank Nighbor, who shared the NHA goal-scoring lead in 1916–17 with Malone, tallying 41 for Ottawa, into their fold, it might put them over the top.

Nighbor was stationed in Toronto with the Royal Flying Corps, so the Toronto owners figured they had a leg up in making a deal with the Senators.

"That Toronto club wants Nighbor very badly," reported the *Ottawa Journal.*

While rumours suggested that they would offer a front-line defenceman such as Harry Cameron or Harry Mummery in exchange, Toronto instead put forward a mere $200 offer for Nighbor. Assuming it was a joke, Ottawa officials simply laughed. Ottawa countered by demanding $1,400 for Nighbor, but Toronto wouldn't ante up that price.

Regardless, Ottawa player-manager Eddie Gerard felt that if the Toronto team could put together a competent system of play to go with their blazing speed, they could easily win the NHL championship.

The inaugural season of the NHL opened on two fronts on December 19, 1917. The Toronto Hockey Club travelled to Montreal to meet the Wanderers at Westmount Arena, while the Canadiens left Montreal to face the Ottawa Senators in the nation's capital at the Laurier Avenue Arena.

Wanderers defenceman Dave Ritchie etched himself forever in the history books when he finished an end-to-end rush and beat Toronto goalie Sammy Hebert at the one-minute mark of the first period for the NHL's first goal. Less than a minute later, Ritchie passed to Jack McDonald, who tallied to make it 2–0, also giving Ritchie the first assist in league history.

The Wanderers led 5–3 after one period and Toronto manager Charlie Querrie had seen enough of Hebert, who was pulled in favour of Art Brooks. Curiously, the Toronto club had dressed two goalies for the game, something that wouldn't be mandatory in the NHL until the 1965–66 season.

The reason why Toronto suited up two netminders was because the team was uncertain which to go with. Neither inspired the confidence of management or the media. "Had either Hebert or Brooks shown any ability to stop shots, the Torontos would have won, as they had the best of the play the greater part of the game," reported the *Montreal Gazette*.

The Toronto World was not as blunt, but arrived at a similar point: "Neither Hebert, who was the Toronto goalkeeper in the earlier part of the game, or Brooks, in the second session, stopped the Wanderers' shots at they might have done."

Wanderers player-manager Art Ross spelled the regulars on occasion and scored one goal in the Wanderers' 10–9 victory.

It would be the only goal that the man for whom the league's scoring trophy is named would ever tally in the NHL.

Harry Hyland finished the game with five goals for the Wanderers, but he ended the night unconscious, knocked out cold after being struck above the eye with a puck that deflected off the stick of Montreal goalie Bert Lindsay.

This new brand of pro hockey was not well-received by the public. Only 700 showed up at the game, even though soldiers in uniform were offered free admission.

Meanwhile in Ottawa, opening night was nearly cancelled. Several Ottawa players refused to suit up, demanding that their contracts be renegotiated before they would play.

An hour prior to game time, Senators goalie Clint Benedict and players Hamby Shore, Jack Darragh, Eddie Lowrey and player-manager Eddie Gerard had still not come to terms with the club. Benedict, Darragh and Gerard claimed they had signed contracts calling for a 20-game season and demanded their pacts be bumped up to take into account the four additional games added to the season. Lowrey had yet to sign any contract and Shore insisted that he was owed back pay.

All but Darragh and Shore had signed by game time. Negotiations with those two players continued after the puck was dropped and

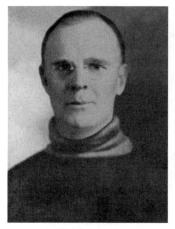 

Eddie Lowrey.   Hamby Shore.

were finalized by the end of the first period. Shore and Darragh were in uniform for the second and third periods of play.

There were 6,000 in the seats, but all the squabbling left the Senators in disarray, leaving the locals little to cheer about as the Canadiens raced to a 3–0 first-period lead en route to a 7–4 win.

Joe Malone scored five goals for Montreal and more than a century later, that remains the franchise record for goals by a player in a road game. On December 22, by virtue of an 11–4 win over Ottawa, Toronto made history, becoming the first (and to date only) NHL team to surrender double digit goals in the first game of the season and then score double digit goals in the second game of the season.

Both Toronto's Corb Denneny and Ottawa's Cy Denneny scored hat tricks, the first time in NHL history that brothers had tallied goals, let alone three each, in the same game.

Frank Nighbor made his season debut for the Senators, under protest from Toronto manager Charlie Querrie, who claimed that the 1916–17 NHA goal-scoring leader hadn't signed a contract. But the two sides had agreed to terms and that was enough to satisfy NHL officials.

Frank Nighbor.

Unable to land Nighbor, the Toronto club set out to solidify their unsettled netminding situation. Hap Holmes, who'd backstopped the Blue Shirts to the 1913–14 Stanley Cup title and Seattle to the 1916–17 Cup crown, began practising with the team. PCHA president Patrick had granted Holmes permission to play in the east, but his rights belonged to the Wanderers, and they sought a King's ransom for Holmes.

"The Torontos will now have to frame up some kind of a trade with the Wanderer club to secure Holmes' services, and it is likely that the Wanderer head will ask for a forward," the *Toronto World* reported. "Holmes was agreeable to cast his lot with the Torontos. Querrie realizes that Holmes is the man to round out the team, and he will work hard to land him."

En route to Toronto for a December 26 game, the train carrying the Canadiens was delayed eight hours just outside of Brockville, Ontario, after the collision of two freight trains. After the wreck was cleared, the team was further delayed when the engine of their own train left the tracks.

There was more trouble afoot in the always unsettled Toronto situation when manager Querrie tendered his resignation on December 28, just three games into the season, claiming interference from the Montreal-based ownership group of the team.

"When I accepted the management of the Toronto team, it was with the understanding that I was to have absolute authority," Querrie told the *Montreal Gazette*. "I have not had a free hand to the extent that was promised me."

Querrie stayed in Toronto as the club travelled to Montreal for its next game under the tutelage of coach Dick Carroll.

Querrie was less forthcoming with the *Toronto World*.

"Who owns the club?" he was asked.

"The Montreal owners of the Toronto Arena," Querrie responded.

Asked to explain the problem he had with ownership, Querrie played coy.

"I am not at liberty to say anything is wrong," Querrie added. "I am not going to Montreal tonight and that is all I can say."

There was a lot of speculation that the source of the unrest and the cause of the resignation of two managers—first Jimmy Murphy and now Querrie—was the constant interference being caused by former owner Eddie Livingstone, who the NHL owners thought they were rid of.

Livingstone adamantly denied any involvement in the Toronto club's woes. "I have absolutely nothing to do with any Toronto team, or any other team," Livingstone told the *Montreal Gazette*. "I have only been at a couple of the practices of the team.

"I am not concerned about the matter at all and it does not make any difference to me who is manager of the team."

Regardless, because of his track record, no one was taking Livingstone at his word. "If Livvy has been interfering, he should have been told to go about his business right at the start," the *Ottawa Journal* wrote. "If he still owns the franchise in the NHA, he has nothing to do with the NHL, which is a new organization and which was formed to get rid of Livvy.

"A new franchise in the new league was given to the Toronto Arena Company and that organization signed up the Toronto NHA players, who were free agents. Livvy has absolutely no jurisdiction over them and he could not prevent any deals for them if he wished.

"However, something unseen is working in connection with the Toronto club when two managers throw up their job, one before the season starts and the other before it is well underway."

After the new Toronto owners conferred with Querrie, he agreed to return to work on New Year's Eve, after an absence of just one game. The new ownership advised Querrie that if Livingstone set foot in Mutual Street Arena, Querrie had their permission to have him removed from the facility immediately.

Just when things were calming down in Toronto, dire circumstances in Montreal threatened the very existence of the fledgling league. The Westmount Arena, home to both the Canadiens and Wanderers, burnt to the ground on January 2, 1918.

Originally opened in 1898 at the corner of St. Catharine Street and Wood Avenue and constructed at a cost of $75,000, the Westmount Arena soon became the centrepiece of hockey in the city. Ten Stanley Cup challenge games were contested over its ice surface. It contained seating for 4,000 fans, but frequently

The Westmount Arena fire, 1917.

as many as 7,000 would cram into the building on game night. Just days prior to the fateful fire, insurance inspectors toured the building and judged it to be up to code.

The cause of the fire was at first unknown. Originally there was some suspicion of foul play, because the fire was thought to have originated within the Wanderers dressing room. The cause was later determined to have been faulty electrical wiring.

The fire began in the early afternoon and firefighters battled the blaze through the night, until 4:00 a.m. the next day. The structure began to collapse within 30 minutes of the start of the fire and the walls were eventually blown out by a boiler explosion.

Quickly realizing that saving the arena was not possible, firefighters focussed on containing the fire and protecting nearby houses. "It is the biggest fire that the firemen of Westmount have been called upon to handle," the Westmount fire brigade chief Moffatt told the *Montreal Gazette*.

Damage was tabulated at $150,000, three times what the building was insured to cover, and among the losses were all the equipment and sticks belonging to the Canadiens and the Wanderers, who were scheduled to play each other that night.

The Canadiens estimated their loss at $1,000, while the Wanderers claimed $950 in losses.

It was immediately announced that Montreal's NHL games would be relocated to the 3,250-seat Jubilee Rink in the mostly French-speaking east-end section of Montreal at St. Catharine and Maisonneuve.

The Wanderers, whose support mainly came from the English-speaking west end of Montreal, expressed reluctance to make such a switch in locales. Wanderers manager Ross was as much concerned by the state of his team as he was about the loss of their home.

"We are badly in need of players and unless we receive help from the other clubs we cannot make a showing in the race for the title," Ross told the *Montreal Gazette*.

A meeting of the NHL board of governors was hastily organized for January 3 at Montreal's Windsor Hotel. "The President [Calder] explained that the meeting had been called at short notice following the destruction by fire of the Montreal Arena," the minutes of the meeting noted.

Lichtenhein echoed Ross' plea for help and took it one step further. Noting that the new players he'd recruited had proven not to be of NHL fettle, Lichtenhein again demanded that the Canadiens hand over Malone, Toronto give them defenceman Harry Mummery and Ottawa supply Crawford or he would quit the league.

His pleas didn't exactly fall on sympathetic ears.

"Owing to the burning down of the Montreal Arena, Sammy Lichtenhein may sell his hockey players," the *Ottawa Journal* noted. "With lemons selling at 10 cents, the owner of the Wanderers should clean up some real coin."

Following what the *Montreal Gazette* described as "a lengthy and stormy session," Calder announced that the Wanderers had resigned from the NHL. Lichtenhein cited operating losses of $2,300 during their brief NHL tenure as the reason why he opted to fold his club.

Informed that he would forfeit the $300 bond put up by each team at the start of the season, Lichtenhein was given 24 hours to reconsider his decision.

A last-ditch effort was made by the management of the Hamilton Arena to convince Lichtenhein to relocate his team to that city, but the Wanderers owner indicated that he couldn't get enough players to make the move to the Ontario steel town.

Just to be certain, the Toronto club showed up at Mutual Street Arena for their slated January 5, 1918 game with the Wanderers. Though the Wanderers, who had dropped out of the league, didn't show for the game—nor did the referees—Toronto went through the motions of shooting the puck into the opposing net to complete the forfeiture.

The same night, the Habs opened play at the tiny bandbox of an ice surface at Jubilee Rink against Ottawa. Both teams struggled to adapt to the limited room between the boards. The first overtime game in NHL history saw the teams play two 10-minute extra periods when tied 5–5 at the end of the third, the Canadiens winning when Joe Malone drove the rebound of a Didier Pitre shot past Ottawa goalie Clint Benedict 7:15 into the second OT session.

A dispersal of the Wanderers players was held. Ottawa received forward Harry Hyland and defenceman Dave Ritchie, while the Canadiens were awarded forwards Jack McDonald and Jack Marks. Toronto was given the NHL rights to goaltender Hap Holmes.

Holmes made his NHL debut January 9 in a 6–4 win over the Canadiens and "added greatly to the strength of the team," the *Montreal Gazette* reported.

Player shortages, however, continued to be an issue. Ottawa lost defenceman Morley Bruce in early January, as he was drafted into the army. At the same time, forward Jack Darragh surprisingly quit the team. "For what, nobody but himself knows," the *Ottawa Journal* noted. Darragh would return to the team a few days later, a financial dispute causing his brief departure.

With so many fit young men off fighting in the Great War, a big part of the problem for the NHL was the lack of available young talent. "It doesn't take a Sherlock Holmes to reason out that the amateur game isn't as fast as it used to be," the *Ottawa Journal* said. "Wanderers withdrew from the NHL because they couldn't get any players to strengthen their team.

"The reason they couldn't get any players to strengthen their team is that the other clubs had no surplus material. And the reason the other clubs had no surplus material is that nothing like the number of young players necessary to keep professional hockey going have been able to make the grade with the pros."

Most of the players in the NHL's inaugural season were long-time pros, still in Canada because married men were exempted from military service. Eight members of the Canadiens were 30 or older, as were five of the Wanderers. Ottawa, with three thirty-somethings and Toronto, with only two, were the younger squads in the league. There were just four rookie players in the entire NHL.

Minus the Wanderers, the NHL reconfigured its schedule for a three-team league, cutting down to a 22-game campaign—14 games in the first half and eight in the second. Teams would alternate, with one playing three times a week and the other two teams twice, the regular season now slated to conclude on March 6.

It seemed that if it weren't for bad luck, the NHL would have no luck at all. And yet they persevered.

"The National Hockey League magnates are running into many obstacles in connection with running off their series this winter, but their bigness is shown by their ability to overcome them all," the *Ottawa Journal* reported.

Officials of the Toronto hockey club suggested publicly that the games involving the disbanded Wanderers should be expunged from the season record. This didn't come as a surprise to many, since Toronto had been the only team to lose to the woeful Wanderers. But Calder wasn't about to entertain such a notion.

"Toronto lost a game here to Wanderers on the merits of the play and there is no reason why they should have this mark against them removed," Calder stated from his office in Montreal.

"Ottawa defeated Wanderers on two occasions on the merits of the play and it would be unfair to Ottawa to take away these games, the only games which the club has won. Canadiens also defeated Wanderers on the merits of the play and are entitled to this victory, as well as to the game awarded them by a default."

Calder noted that for all the crowing in Toronto, no paperwork had been filed with the league to eliminate the Wanderers from the league standings.

"I have received no official protest against either the schedule arrangements or the ruling on the Wanderers games from the Toronto club, but there will be no change in either," Calder said.

Ed Sheppard, president of the Montreal Arena Company, announced on January 9 that the Westmount Arena would not be rebuilt until after the Great War, the cost of steel during wartime being too prohibitive. In fact, they would wait much longer than anticipated to construct the new rink, which only opened in 1924, as the fabled Forum. The Canadiens players agreed as a team to take a $1,000 deduction in salary to offset the costs to the team by the loss of their equipment in the fire.

The Denneny siblings made history again on January 14 when both Toronto's Corb and the Senators' Cy fired hat tricks in Ottawa's 9–6 win.

The Canadiens and Toronto were establishing themselves as the class of the league. "Torontos, with youth and speed, are the team to beat," opined the *Ottawa Journal.*

Montreal felt that the Toronto team completely lacked class, and accused them of being brutes on home ice. "The Toronto team, according to the Canadiens players, are a dangerous outfit," reported the *Montreal Star.* "Dangerous in more ways that one, for in their own city they play a brand of hockey not attempted by any other club in the league. Any other team who tried it would land up in jail.

"In Toronto, however, the Blue Shirts get away with it themselves, but woe to any foreign player who attempts to retaliate. It is the bench at once, and the presence of a burly policeman behind the penalty box is a grim reminder that the jail awaits all unruly hockey players in Toronto—who do not belong to the home team."

The Canadiens offered up an injury report from a recent trip to the Queen City as evidence of the dirty deeds committed by the Toronto club. Newsy Lalonde was nursing two loose teeth. Malone was ailing with a painful back and a sore leg, while Hall's wrist, where it had been whacked by the stick of Toronto forward Alf Skinner, was about twice its normal size.

According to Canadiens manager Kennedy, the intimidation extended beyond the boards. He accused Toronto police of harassing and threatening his players during games at Mutual Street Arena. "Two officers were continually behind the penalty bench," Kennedy complained to the *Toronto World*. "And every time one of our players drew a penalty, he was told by an officer not to repeat the offence or arrest would follow. 'The patrol wagon will soon be backing up for you,' was the expression one officer used to a player.

"[Billy] Couture came very nearly [to] being arrested after his run in with [Toronto captain Ken] Randall, for he spoke back sharply to the officer who cautioned him. If it had not been for [Canadiens captain] Lalonde, Couture would have gone to jail.

"The result of this was that our players were afraid to move. The Toronto players get away with everything, and practically every player on our team is marked. Lalonde had his eye split open by [Reg] Noble; [Bert] Corbeau's thumb is swollen to twice its natural size as a result of a deliberate slash by [Corb] Denneny, and Malone is limping as the result of a slash across the knee. If a check which Randall aimed at Couture's face had landed, Couture would have been disfigured for life."

The Canadiens vowed to seek out a grudge-match type victory the next time the Toronto team visited Montreal.

Querrie viewed the Canadiens as nothing more than crybabies. "Whatever rough play there was, was instigated by the Montreal players," the Toronto manager told the *Toronto Daily Star*. "Kennedy is a poor loser."

When the rough stuff continued and spilled into an Ottawa-Montreal game on January 12th where the Canadiens' Lalonde butt-ended Senators forward Cy Denneny in the face while Denneny was being held by a game official after they'd fought, Calder determined that it was time to take action. Lalonde got a $15 fine for receiving a match penalty and Calder tacked on another $10 for the butt end.

"As far as the fight went, it was 50–50 as to who was to blame," Calder told the *Ottawa Journal*. "There was no justification or excuse for the action of Lalonde in striking Denneny while the referees were holding him."

"Lalonde should get the gate for the season," the *Ottawa Journal* reported. "He is a hindrance to clean sport and the quicker he is out, the better for the game."

Calder issued a warning to all the teams that this sort of conduct would bring about severe punishment.

Even though Montreal posted a decisive 5–1 home-ice verdict over Toronto on January 19, they lost their captain Lalonde for several weeks after he suffered a gashed right foot when accidentally kicked by the skate of Toronto defenceman Harry Mummery.

Four nights later, on the train home from Ottawa following a 4–3 loss, several Canadiens players fell ill with food poisoning, blaming it on the tomato soup they ate in a restaurant in Ottawa prior to boarding the train.

Edouard "Newsy" Lalonde.

Despite the myriad problems facing the fledgling league, support for it continued to grow during these early days, and from a variety of quarters. These included those headed for the trenches of Europe. In England with the

228th Battalion, Corporal Goldie Prodger, a member of the Canadiens' 1915–16 Stanley Cup winner, wrote home to raise awareness of the importance of hockey even during wartime.

"Even if we are at war with an enemy that threatens our very existence, it is no reason why the great winter sport should be allowed to die," Prodger wrote. "In fact, just such diversions are required at this time to keep the minds of those at home away from the horrors of war."

Those pros who'd enlisted were fighting on the front lines and were paying the same horrific price as the soldiers who weren't hockey stars. Leth Graham, who'd played with Ottawa in the NHA, was victimized by a German mustard gas attack and though he survived and returned to play in the NHL after the war, he was never able to be more than a spare, capable of playing only a few minutes per game.

The Senators moved to accommodate recovering war veterans during their games, putting aside a block of free tickets made available to the patients of the Military Hospitals Commission Command who were under treatment at Ottawa's Sir Sanford Fleming Convalescent Home. "To those, most of whom have lost forever the joy of freedom of action, a game like hockey has a particular charm," Miss M. McLaren, matron of the convalescent home, told the *Ottawa Journal*.

The Canadiens sought permission from the league and from the Senators to move a Montreal-Ottawa game to Quebec, as he was certain that, with former Quebec players Dave Ritchie, Joe Malone and Rusty Crawford in uniform between the two teams, the game would draw a sell-out crowd.

The saga of Frank Nighbor's lost season continued. He'd been limited to two games with the Senators due to his military commitments and in late January, travelled to Pittsburgh to play for the Royal Flying Corps hockey team. "The Ottawa fellows have had a great deal of hard luck," Kennedy said. "It always comes in bunches."

Calder felt badly that circumstances were preventing Nighbor, one of the game's best players, from suiting up. "It is unfortunate that he is being kept out of hockey," Calder told the *Ottawa Citizen*.

Meanwhile, even though the Canadiens had won five of their first six games and eight of their first 10 contests, Querrie scoffed at suggestions that Montreal was the team to beat for the NHL title. "Canadiens with the addition of Hall and Malone from Quebec looked like winners in a canter, but they are having their troubles," Querrie said.

Querrie continued his tough talk on the eve of their January 26 game at Ottawa. "The fans have the impression that Canadiens have cinched the honours in the first series of the pro hockey race," Querrie told the *Toronto World*. "Such is not the case. We have only lost one more game than the Canadiens and have a chance to beat them out yet."

Then his team took a pratfall, getting dumped by the Senators. Ottawa grabbed a 6–0 lead and only a trio of third-period goals made the final scoreline a bit closer.

Unable to land Nighbor, Querrie, who'd also been pursuing Sarnia amateur forward Jack Adams since early January, set his sights on rugged former Wanderers defenceman Sprague Cleghorn, who was recovering from a fractured ankle. But Cleghorn proved to have more serious issues to deal with. He was in court, where he was acquitted of assaulting his wife, who'd accused him of beating her with one his crutches. Querrie was also attempting to get the name of former Canadiens forward Tommy Smith on a contract,

Jack Adams.

and there was speculation the team was also after Ross, the ex-player/manager of the Wanderers. Eventually, Toronto settled on picking up veteran forward Jack Marks, who'd been dropped by the Canadiens after they acquired him when the Wanderers folded, but found that the old-time star no longer had much left to give on the ice.

Canadiens manager George Kennedy was once again outraged by the underhanded play of the Toronto team. "The [Montreal] players got a terrible mauling and one they will not forget when Toronto comes here Saturday night," he said. "Joe Malone, as clean a player as there is in hockey, was knocked out cold with a butt end. Lalonde was slashed across the knee so badly that he had to quit the game. One of Hall's knees is twice the size of the other. Early in the game, Corbeau got a poke in the stomach that left him sick for the rest of the match. When Toronto had the game cinched, they deliberately went out to cripple our players."

The Habs clinched first-half honours in the NHL standings with a 5–2 win January 30 at Ottawa, as Joe Malone scored four goals.

Coming to Montreal for a meaningless February 2 game after the Canadiens had already clinched the first-half title, Toronto players Reg Noble and Harry Cameron lit out on the town the night before the game and sampled a bit too much of the Montreal nightlife. Each was fined $100 by the team for breaking training rules and when Noble protested, he was fined an additional $100 and suspended for the game.

A 10–4 record earned the Canadiens the first-half title and an automatic berth in the NHL playoff at the end of the season. Montreal did it right at both ends of the rink, scoring a league-high 81 goals while allowing a league-low 47 tallies. The Canadiens were the only team in the league with a positive goal differential during the first half.

Malone finished the first half of the season with 34 goals, 10 more than any other player.

Ottawa got some hopeful news as the first half of the season wound down. Frank Nighbor had secured a leave from his duties as a mechanic with the Royal Flying Corps and would be joining the Senators for the second half. There were changes afoot in both Ottawa and Toronto. Ottawa handed Rusty Crawford his release and named Harry Hyland, who'd gained leave from his job in Montreal and would be available for the entire second half of the season, as a player-assistant coach to player-manager Eddie Gerard. Toronto signed Crawford and also finally inked promising amateur forward Jack Adams from Sarnia, who the team had been pursuing for a month.

As the home crowd chanted "Bring on Nighbor," he scored a goal and an assist to help Ottawa get the second half underway via a 6–3 February 6 win over the Canadiens, leaving the *Ottawa Journal* suitably impressed, predicting that the Senators wouldn't lose another game the rest of the way. "The team as it stands today is the class of the league in all departments," the paper reported. "The Senators laid over the Canadiens like a tent in the last game, and if the same kind had been played by them during the first half they, and not Canadiens, would have been winners."

Others were equally impressed. "Those Ottawa fellows... they'll bear watching for the balance of the season if I am not greatly mistaken," Montreal Canadiens manager-owner George Kennedy told the *Ottawa Citizen*. "I'm glad to see Nighbor back in the game. No one admires him more than I."

Originally, it appeared that wartime fuel conservation regulations that were implemented requiring all places of public amusement to be closed every Monday from February 18 through March 25 would lead to the rescheduling of a pair of NHL games, but hockey was granted an exemption to the order.

"President [Frank] Calder of the NHL has been notified by Assistant Fuel Controller Peterson that no change need be made in the schedule of the league on account of the coal conservation order," the *Montreal Star* reported. "It was suggested that the

Monday games of the league would be put back, because the rinks could not be regarded as places of amusement. Mr. Peterson rules that the NHL games are regarded as events excepted in the order, because the tickets for them have been printed."

There were other difficulties arising in hockey south of the border that were created partly by the goings-on of the NHL. A newly formed National Amateur Hockey Association in the United States was declared to be a pro outfit due to the presence of Raymie Skilton and Jerry Geran with the Boston team. Both had played for the Wanderers before the Montreal team folded.

"Jerry Geran, who tried out with the Wanderers, and who played a couple of games early in the season, is back in Boston, playing in the new hockey league," the *Ottawa Journal* noted. "And still the teams down there claim to be amateur. Fine stuff."

Unhappy with the work of Clint Benedict between the pipes, and feeling he was in need of a rest, Ottawa tried out Bert McAndrews from the Pembroke amateurs in practice, but instead acquired Sammy Hebert on loan from Toronto to serve as insurance behind Benedict. There was also talk that the Senators were pursuing former Wanderers manager Art Ross to bolster their defence, but he felt that they were barking up the wrong tree.

Raymie Skilton with the Boston Amature Club.

"I'd like to be on the ice with the Ottawa club... for I think the Senators are the class of the league but the notice is too short," Ross said. "The only thing I could stop is a streetcar. It is quite true that I told the Ottawa management some time ago that I would help them out in a pinch, but I'm not in shape to play hockey at once."

Unable to land Ross, the Senators went back to the future, signing defenceman Horace Merrill, a member of their 1914–15 NHA championship club, and releasing Dave Ritchie.

Meanwhile, the Canadiens were attempting to convince ex-Wanderers forward Odie Cleghorn to join their club, but he'd been warned by the military board that he'd forfeit his exemption were he to don a pair of skates.

The Wanderers were long gone, but a group of former Wanderers gathered to play a charity game to benefit the Tobacco Fund, a non-profit group that raised money to purchase cigarettes for the soldiers fighting the Great War. Among the old-time Wanderers who signed on to play were goalie Riley Hern, Jack Marshall, Dickie Boon, Jimmy Gardner and Tom Melville from their Stanley Cup-winning teams of the early 1900s, while players from the 1917–18 NHL Wanderers included George O'Grady, Kenny Thompson and Ross also participated.

With the Canadiens stumbling in the second half, opening it with consecutive lopsided losses after capturing the first-half title, there were people willing to suggest that the Canadiens were laying down on the job—not that they were throwing games, but that they were performing like a fat and happy bunch, knowing they were assured of a playoff spot. Regardless, these accusations sent Kennedy off on a tangent. "It's all very well for the dyspeptic anvil chorus to say, 'Canadiens are playing indifferent hockey in this half,'" Kennedy told the *Montreal Herald*. "But they overlook the fact that it is costing me money. For one thing, I have hired one more player than I used in the first half and that will cost something over $300. I won the first half without this player, and it's obvious if I was not anxious to win the second half, I wouldn't have hired him. Losing games hurts the gates. The two losses we have sustained will affect the gate receipts to the extent of $1,500."

It was well-known within hockey circles that gambling on NHL games was rampant, and it wasn't uncommon for sums between $4,000–5,000 to change hands in wagers on key games. Prior to a playoff series, newspapers would post the odds on each game and declare which team was the betting favourite. And the infamous Black Sox scandal, in which eight members of the Chicago White Sox were accused of conspiring with gamblers to throw the World Series, was only a year away from occurring, so to suggest that there was no connection between pro sports and gambling was pure folly.

Still, Kennedy was adamant that there was no such back-room dealing taking place with his team, nor had he ever seen any evidence of such shenanigans in all his years in the game of hockey.

"It's easy to talk about fixing games but I never heard of it being done—not in this league, anyway," Kennedy said. "If there was any fixing, you can bet I wouldn't have my team dropping into last place right at the start of the second series. The last-place teams don't cause any rush in the direction of the box office."

A Montreal-Ottawa tilt on February 16 brought fast pace to new levels. The two teams played the third period almost without stoppage, finishing the 20-minute frame in 21 minutes, 51 and three-fifths seconds.

The Canadiens were winless in three trips to Toronto when they arrived for a February 18 game at Mutual Street Arena. Looking to change their luck, the Montreal players decided to live out opposite day.

Instead of leaving the morning of the game, they took the train to Toronto the night before. Rather than walking to the rink, they took the streetcar. The time of the pre-game meal was moved up an hour. They stayed up upon arriving in Toronto in the morning, opting for an afternoon nap.

It worked. Montreal won the game in a rout by a 9–0 count, as Canadiens goalie Georges Vezina posted the first shutout ever recorded in NHL history. Joe Malone reached the 40-goal plateau in this game, something no NHL player would again do until the 1929–30 season.

After beating Toronto in successive games in mid-February, Kennedy was beginning to doubt that the Toronto club was going to offer much competition. "Ottawa will be the team to beat, in my opinion," Kennedy told the *Ottawa Citizen*. "My players are determined on winning the championship without the necessity of a playoff."

Canadiens captain Newsy Lalonde was called home to Cornwall, Ontario, in late February by the illness of his father and ended up saving the lives of his parents, wife and niece. Returning to their house in the evening to find it filled with coal gas, Lalonde immediately threw open all the windows and doors, and summoned a physician to attend to his victimized family, all of whom would have been asphyxiated without his quick action.

More history was made February 27 at Quebec, as Ottawa beat Montreal 3–1 in the first neutral-site game in NHL history. There were 2,500 in attendance and not a single penalty was called during the game.

Hoping to motivate the Canadiens on the eve of their March 2 game at Toronto, the Ottawa brass dangled a $2,000 cash incentive in front of them for a win, as that would propel Ottawa into the playoffs ahead of their Queen City rivals. Senators management felt it would be money well spent, seeing as a playoff appearance for Ottawa would have been worth $6,000 in gate receipts. But the Canadiens didn't make any friends in Canada's capital city when they arrived in Toronto minus Joe Malone and Didier Pitre, two-thirds of their top forward line, citing illness as the reason behind their absence.

In the early going, it looked as if Ottawa's promised bonus helped to motivate the Canadiens. Despite their depleted lineup, and much to the delight of Ottawa fans, who besieged local tele-graph offices for updates, and to the Senators players, crowded into their dressing room at the Laurier Avenue Rink, getting live updates from Mutual Street Arena via telephone, Montreal led 3–2 in the second period. But Toronto tied it before the end of the frame and rallied for a 5–3 victory and the second-half title.

Ottawa whipped Toronto 9–3 in a meaningless season ender March 6, but some found the game worth taking in. Interested spectators at the game were Canadiens manager George Kennedy and Montreal players Newsy Lalonde and Joe Malone, doing a bit of scouting prior to their upcoming playoff series for the NHL title.

The race couldn't have finished much closer. Toronto won with a 5–3 record, the Senators finished 4–4 and the Canadiens brought up the rear at 3–5. Even the goal differentials were remarkably close. Toronto scored 37 and allowed 34, Ottawa was dead even at 35–35, while the Habs tallied 34 times and let in 37 goals.

THE PLAYOFFS

As Toronto and the Montreal Canadiens prepared to clash for the NHL championship and the right to represent the fledgling league in its first Stanley Cup series, the experts were just about split as to which club would cop the NHL title. Toronto was the faster team, capable of putting together displays of brilliant hockey, but the seasoned Canadiens, who had played in the previous two Stanley Cup finals, were much more consistent performers.

"They are a team of players who, as a rule, stick to strict training and seldom wander from the beaten path," the *Ottawa Journal* noted of the Canadiens. "On the other hand, the Blues are a wild and erratic lot. They have a whole lot of hockey ability in their makeup but cannot be depended upon at any time. At least four of their players are continually breaking training, and have been known on several occasions to be in anything but fit condition to play the game."

Harvey Pulford and Charlie McKinley, both of Ottawa, were named to officiate the series, seeing as neither had any ties to either of the teams or cities involved in the series.

Montreal manager George Kennedy also announced that if the Canadiens won the NHL title, the Stanley Cup games would be played at Toronto's Mutual Street Arena and Ottawa's Laurier Avenue Rink, also referred to as Dey's Rink, rather than Montreal's tiny Jubilee Rink. "It's unlikely that either Seattle, Vancouver or Portland would ever consider coming east to play in the Jubilee Rink in Montreal, for outside of the fact that the rink is not modern, its seating capacity would never make the series a paying proposition," the *Toronto Mail and Empire* reported.

A *Montreal Herald* reader took it upon himself to pick the first all-star team in NHL history and send his selections along to *Herald* sports editor Elmer Ferguson. The reader selected three Canadiens—Georges Vezina in goal, Bert Corbeau on defence, Lalonde on left wing and Didier Pitre on right wing, completing the squad with Ottawa's Gerard on defence and Nighbor at centre. Curiously, no Toronto players were chosen and neither was Canadiens centre Joe Malone, who'd tallied a league-leading 44 goals in 20 games.

Almost immediately, there was bickering over the dates for the home-and-home two-game total goals series for NHL supremacy. Toronto's Charlie Querrie wanted the final game to be played in Toronto, while Montreal's George Kennedy insisted that decision was up to NHL president Frank Calder. Querrie felt that a coin toss should be held to give the team that won the toss the option of which game in the series they wanted played at their rink.

"We'll play on the dates set by the president or not at all," Kennedy grumbled. "Canadiens have a better record than Torontos all through and if the blues don't want to play we'll be willing to call the series off, take the championship and go ahead with the Stanley Cup games.

"I was not consulted about the dates and I haven't been officially notified what the dates are. I don't know what Querrie's moaning about. I guess it's a habit."

Almost on cue, Querrie got into habit, as Kennedy would say, insisting the Toronto team would play an exhibition series with Ottawa instead of facing the Canadiens if the second game of the series was not held in Toronto.

It's incredible in this time and age to consider that an NHL team might be willing to walk away from a chance to play for the Stanley Cup, but it certainly speaks to the sort of outlaw mentality that ruled pro sports of the day.

Try and imagine the current owner of an NHL team seeking to dictate terms of a playoff series to NHL commissioner Gary Bettman. He'd certainly hear nothing of such nonsense, and as it turned out, neither would Calder.

"Querrie will do no such thing," Calder said. "I will certainly not permit any such series with Ottawa as he suggests, if Querrie runs out on the Stanley Cup series. If he flatly refuses to play these games, that, of course, is up to him, though it will seriously jeopardize his position in the league, and might result in his ejectment.

"I have had no official notification from Querrie, however, except that he wishes the dates changed. I selected dates from a practical point of view, and see no reason for changing them."

Querrie finally relented to the dates set by Calder. Toronto would play host to Montreal in Game 1 of the series on March 11, with the two teams then playing in Montreal on March 13. The Canadiens were listed as 8–5 favourites to win the title.

The Senators were not left out, however, as both they and the Canadiens agreed to play a home and home series after the conclusion of the NHL playoffs, with the winner grabbing 60 per cent of the gate and the loser 40 per cent.

Word came from Ottawa that Senators forward Harry Hyland had enlisted in the Canadian

Gorges Boucher.

Forces and would be headed to join the fighting in the Great War in May. Ottawa was already scouting out talent for the 1918–19 season and were said to like the looks of a group of local amateurs that included Aurel Joliat, Jack MacKell, Joe Matte and the Boucher brothers, Billy and Frank, younger siblings of current Senators player Georges Boucher.

It was reported that Eddie Livingstone, erstwhile former owner of the Toronto franchise, would earn between $5,000-$6,000 per the deal he'd reached with the new owners of the team.

NHL PLAYOFFS: GAME ONE
March 11, 1918
Montreal Canadiens 3 at Toronto Hockey Club 7

After the back and forth bickering between the two teams over which club would get to play host to the second game of the set, it finally opened at Toronto's Mutual Street Arena. In what was described by the *Montreal Gazette* as "the greatest exhibition of professional hockey witnessed [in Toronto] in years," Toronto got off to a winning start in the NHL playoffs, whipping Montreal 7–3 on March 11 to the delight of 3,000 fans at Mutual Street Arena Gardens. Toronto sought to utilize its speed advantage to put the Canadiens on the back foot. "The pace was dazzling from the outset, the players of both teams digging into the fray with a do-or-die spirit," *the Gazette* reported. "The Torontos had a margin of the play in the early stages, and [Canadiens goalie Georges] Vezina was called upon to stop many dangerous shots."

Toronto forward Harry Meeking was the star of the night, netting a hat trick. Toronto rookie Jack Adams netted his first goal as a pro, but his joy was short-lived. After the game, he learned that he had been called to military service.

Montreal tired as the game wore on, struggling to deal with Toronto's speed, especially that of defenceman Harry Cameron, whose rushing of the puck was a constant feature of the play. He scored once and his puck-moving skills led to a pair of Toronto goals that he set up.

The tension of the moment often got the better of both teams, and discipline frequently waned. "Thrills and spills featured the proceedings, the checking being fierce," *the Gazette* noted. "Numerous penalties were indicted, all of which were deserved, as the player carrying the puck was a target for much abuse."

Toronto grabbed a four-goal lead in the two-game, total goals series for the NHL title. "Canadiens were outskated, outplayed and outguessed from the start," Elmer Ferguson reported in the *Montreal Herald.*

GAME TWO

March 13, 1918
Toronto Hockey Club 3 at Montreal Canadiens 4

Heading to Montreal for the second game, the fear was that Mother Nature might have implications in the outcome, since the Jubilee Rink was a natural ice surface. "Weather conditions promise to be mild, and with the rink packed, the ice is likely to be soft and heavy," the *Toronto Star* assessed. "This will hamper a fast-skating team like Toronto, accustomed to hard artificial ice."

As it turned out, the weather report was flawed. It was cold in Montreal, and the take on this game was completely different from the assessment of the series opener. "The match was one of the poorest exhibitions of hockey witnessed in Montreal this season," reported the *Toronto World,* accusing the Canadiens of adopting rough house tactics when it became apparent that the series was not theirs to win.

"Although it started well, it developed into a contest of brute strength, and the Canadiens' chances faded away when they undertook to make the visitors quit by roughing it with them on every possible occasion."

A capacity crowd of 3,250 crammed into the Jubilee Rink and booed the Toronto club from the moment they took the ice, but to no avail. The Canadiens simply couldn't overcome the four-goal deficit they faced and though they won the game, lost out 10–7 in the total goals series.

"Torontos played the puck more than the man and took the bumps handed to them without relenting to any great extent," the *Toronto World* noted. "This accounted greatly in their favour and with the good use of substitutes, they were enabled to keep up with Canadiens at all stages of the play."

One of those subs, forward Rusty Crawford, proved the star of the night for Toronto. "Crawford, who was released by Ottawa early in the season, was the most brilliant player on the visiting team," *the World* assessed. "He accounted for two of their goals and played a clever defensive game as well."

Several of the Toronto players were also left down for the count by the ongoing physical assault of the Canadiens. Ken Randall was injured early in the game, gashed for a four-stitch cut to the head after he was caught in a sandwich between Canadiens players Joe Hall and Newsy Lalonde. Randall was unable to continue. Jack Adams' head was cut to ribbons and Crawford was battered from head to foot. Harry Cameron was

Bert Corbeau.

left hobbled by a slash from Bert Corbeau. Harry Meeking was knocked unconscious by a Billy Couture check and Alf Skinner was also rendered senseless by a hit. Even goalie Hap Holmes suffered broken teeth during the game.

Adams, Meeking and Randall were so badly cut up that they required surgical attention upon returning to Toronto. Adams was messed up to a point that his sister, a nurse at the hospital, at first did not recognize her brother. Dripping with blood as he came to the bench after one shift, Adams, who'd just been called to military service, joked, "A few more games like this and I'll sure be eligible for Class E [deferment]."

An interested spectator at the game in Montreal was none other than former owner Eddie Livingstone, who offered a $100 bonus for the Toronto player he felt checked the best during the game, made a bold claim that he still owned the Toronto club and anticipated garnering a significant stipend due to his share of the gate receipts from the NHL playoff series.

While Toronto was being crowned in the east, the Pacific Coast Hockey Association was also contesting its playoff, pitting the defending Stanley Cup champion Seattle Metropolitans against the Vancouver Millionaires.

First-place Seattle was anticipated to defend its title and when the Mets got late goal from Bernie Morris to record a 2–2 in Game 1 in front of 8,000 at Vancouver on March 11, things certainly look likely to go their way.

Even the *Vancouver Daily World* seemed to see it that way. "It was a technical victory for Seattle," the paper reported. "This may sound an unusual statement, but it must be remembered that the Metropolitans were playing on foreign ice, and an even break to them was all that the most sanguine member of the invading team hoped for.

"When the Millionaires step on the ice at Seattle [for Game 2] and [seek to] nose out the league leaders, they will be [trying to] overcome a big handicap. Seattle has a reputation of being the hardest team in the league to whip on home ice."

Bookmakers were in agreement, offering 10–7 odds on the Mets to cop the crown.

With 3,500 spectators jammed into the Seattle Arena on the night of March 13 for Game 2 of the two-game total goals set, there was a festive atmosphere, as the locals were confident that the Mets, the first American-based team to win the Stanley Cup, were poised to move on and defend their title. "With horns and every other conceivable mechanical invention for making noise, [the fans] fairly lifted the roof from its foundations," the *Seattle Star* reported.

But Vancouver had other ideas. At the 11:10 mark of the second period, Mickey MacKay fed a pass to Barney Stanley, who chipped the puck past Seattle goalie Norman [Hec] Fowler for the only goal of the contest, giving the Millionaires a 3–2 series triumph. It was Vancouver's first win all season at Seattle. "It was just like playing 60 minutes overtime," Millionaires defenceman Si Griffis said of the tightly contested game.

"Gloom marked the face of each Seattle fan as the crowd made its way from the building," the *Seattle Star* reported. "So sure had the Seattle team been of winning that the players had their luggage all packed and were ready to depart. Their visions of a trip to Toronto and a slice of the world's series coin were rudely shattered."

Instead, it was Vancouver that had captured the PCHA title and earned the right to head eastward and compete with the champions of the newfound NHL for the Stanley Cup.

"Great satisfaction was expressed by the members of the [Vancouver] team on Torontos winning the NHL championship," the *Vancouver Daily World* reported. "The world's series games will now be played on artificial ice, which will give the Millionaires a much better advantage than if the games were played in Montreal [on the natural ice surface at the Jubilee Rink]."

THE STANLEY CUP

While the Toronto Hockey Club was busy dispatching the Montreal Canadiens, who'd represented the NHA in the 1916–17 Stanley Cup, from the playoff picture in the NHL final, on the west coast the Vancouver Millionaires were punching the defending Stanley Cup champion Seattle Metropolitans out of the hunt in the Pacific Coast Hockey Association final.

Long before any other major league sport, hockey's championship had become a true East-West showdown. The PCHA champions and NHA champions began facing off for Lord Stanley's mug in 1914, and Vancouver had first taken the Cup westward by beating the Ottawa Senators in the 1914–15 final series.

Major League Baseball wouldn't go to the west coast until the 1950s, a few years before the National Basketball Association and about a decade after the National Football League. Even the Grey Cup didn't have an east-west showdown until 1921. In that regard, hockey was way ahead of the curve.

The Stanley Cup.

Where the final would be played was another matter. They did not decide it as is done today, with the series split between the winning teams: the difficulty of long-distance travel made this impossible. Nor were all arenas created equal, or up to the task of hosting a championship series. Montreal manager George Kennedy fully expected that his Canadiens would be in the final; but he also knew that the team's tiny Jubilee Rink could not host the series, so he made arrangements which allowed the series to be played in Vancouver. The PCHA was willing to guarantee the Canadiens $7,000 in gate receipts as part of the deal, and both sides agreed that the 1919 Cup final series would have come east. But when Toronto upset the Habs, this point became moot. Mutual Street Arena in Toronto was a palace complete with an artificial ice surface, well-suited for playing host to a series of this magnitude.

The Vancouver squad that would come east—the two leagues alternated, with the Cup final series being held in the eastern city in even-numbered years and the western city in odd-numbered years—was a powerhouse bunch. Five players remained from the 1914–15 Cup winners and PCHA president Frank Patrick was manager of the club.

The roster included three PCHA all-stars in goalie Hugh Lehman and forwards Fred [Cyclone] Taylor and Duncan [Mickey] MacKay. Taylor had set a league record by topping the PCHA with 32 goals to earn the nod as the league's MVP.

The Vancouver club left by train from their home city at 5:00 p.m. on March 14, slated to get to Toronto via Chicago. Negotiations on how the series would be played and who would be involved with the games began while the Millionaires were in the midst of their journey.

Along with wiring congratulations to the Toronto club on their win, Patrick also indicated that the PCHA offered to play six-man hockey and drop its rover position if the NHL would agree to their deferred penalty rules and allow kicking of the puck. Vancouver also sought to use a referee from their own league during the Stanley Cup series. PCHA official George Irvine made the trip east with the team.

Toronto was seeking an allowance to suit up players Jack Adams and Rusty Crawford. Both were acquired following the February 1 player deadline to make them eligible to perform in the Stanley Cup final, so permission from Vancouver to use the two players would be required. Crawford (two goals) and Adams (one goal) were both valuable contributors to Toronto's win over the Canadiens in the NHL final, so the teams brass considered them significant additions in the bid for the Stanley Cup.

While awaiting word on these deals, the Toronto players held a team meeting and decided that regardless of whether they were permitted to play, Adams and Crawford would both be allotted a cut of the players' share of the Stanley Cup gate receipts. Under the rules of the day, players from both teams were guaranteed a share of the gate from the first three games of the series. Ticket prices for the Stanley Cup games in Toronto ranged from 50 cents to $2, but purchasers were required to buy tickets for a minimum of three games. Bookmakers established Toronto as 2–1 favourites to win the Stanley Cup.

Since Taylor was a long-time star in the nation's capital, there was anxiousness on the part of the Ottawa fans to see their former hero in person. The Senators offered the Vancouver team a $1,000 guarantee if the Millionaires would play an exhibition game in Ottawa while in the east for the Stanley Cup series.

Perhaps it was an oversight, or perchance it was overconfidence, but when the Vancouver club packed for the trip to Toronto, they forgot to bring one vital package—the Stanley Cup that had gone west with the Metropolitans the year before. It was left behind in Vancouver, on display at the Henry Birks & Sons Jewellery Store. The Millionaires guaranteed the Stanley Cup would be shipped east after the series if Vancouver was vanquished by Toronto.

Meanwhile, there was consternation in Toronto that the players had celebrated their NHL title a little too enthusiastically. "Grave rumours are going the rounds to the effect that certain players on the team have not been observing the strictest rules of training," the *Ottawa Journal* reported. "It is reported

that manager [Charlie] Querrie is seriously considering dropping them altogether if the coast champions will agree to allowing Crawford and Adams to play in the series."

Vancouver arrived in Toronto on March 19, five days after
their departure. Asked whether he'd permit Crawford and
Adams to play, Patrick offered a terse, one-word response: "No."
Patrick felt it would set a bad precedent for future Stanley Cup
series were they to ignore the rules.

Upon getting to the Queen City, the Vancouver party
checked into the King Edward Hotel and then embarked for
Mutual Street Arena, where the Millionaires put in a strenuous
practice in hopes of shaking the rust from their five-day trek over
the rails prior to the March 20 opener of the best-of-five series.

Meanwhile, on the eve of the series, Toronto goalie Harry
(Hap) Holmes was struck near the eye with a puck and thus
would enter the fray for Lord Stanley's mug sporting a badly
discoloured eye on his own mug.

The odd-numbered games in the series—Games 1, 3, and
5—were to be played under NHL rules. Games 2 and 4 would
be conducted by PCHA rules. Under the PCHA rulebook the
ice surface was divided into three equal portions by two blue
lines. No offside was called in the mid-ice block, the neutral
zone, and forward passing was allowed in this area of the ice, but
in either of the other two zones, the NHL offside rule applied,
prohibiting attacking players from being ahead of the puck.

The PCHA also played seven-man hockey, utilizing a rover,
and when a player was penalized, he would not be replaced on
the ice, creating a power-play situation for the other team.

Patrick felt his team's conditioning would win the day for
them. "We expect to go through the full game without a change,
unless it is for a penalty," he told the *Vancouver Daily World*.

The speculation was that Vancouver had little chance to
emerge victorious. "It is hardly likely that the Vancouver team
will win the world's series from Toronto Blues," was the opinion of the *Ottawa Journal*, "for neither the eastern nor western

organization has yet been able to develop a team of super hockey players able to triumph over the terrific handicap under which a team plays after crossing three thousand miles of continent, and playing before an absolutely strange crowd on strange ice.

"No team can maintain its finely adjusted physical edge on such a long journey."

Oddsmakers disagreed and after watching the Vancouver team at practice, dropped Toronto's odds of winning the series down to 7–5.

Playing Game 1 under the rules of the NHL meant that the teams would skate six aside and that the Millionaires would be required to adjust their lineup to get leading scorer Taylor, normally the rover, into their starting lineup.

The Vancouver team that arrived to contest the Stanley Cup included the following:

LEO COOK, CENTRE

The younger brother of Vancouver captain Lloyd Cook, Leo was a speedy player and a classy stickhandler, but at 5–9 and 165 pounds, lacked the size to be a regular in the pro ranks.

A journeyman, Cook skated in seven cities in five pro seasons—Vancouver, Victoria and Spokane of the PCHA and Saskatoon, Moose Jaw, Regina and Edmonton in the WCHL.

Cook's career was bookended by suspensions. He was banned from the Alberta Senior League in 1912 for known association with professionals. And in 1931, Cook was suspended for life from the California Hockey League after assaulting an official.

LLOYD COOK, DEFENCE

Captain of the Vancouver club, Cook was a rookie when Vancouver won the Stanley Cup in 1914–15. A productive offensive player who thought constantly of initiating the attack and leading a rush toward the opposition goal, Cook scored five goals in a 1916 game and led all PCHA defencemen in scoring with 19–11–30 totals in 1922–23. He was a six-time PCHA all-star. In the summers, Cook was a cattle farmer in his home of Taber, Alberta.

Known as a stalwart defender, Cook signed with the expansion Boston Bruins in 1924, but at 34 was past his prime and saw duty in just four NHL games. Heading to the U.S. west coast, Cook helped the minor-pro California League to blossom, playing and coaching, as well as owning teams in Los Angeles and San Francisco.

SI GRIFFIS, DEFENCE

Griffis first won the Stanley Cup with the 1906–07 Kenora Thistles, and one of his teammates on that club, Billy McGimsie, sung the praises of Griffis in a 1960 interview. "Si could do anything with a hockey stick and a puck," McGimsie claimed. "He could play any position and he could play it well."

Equipped with blazing speed, Griffis began his career as a rover and later moved back to defence. At 6–1 and 195 pounds, he was a behemoth in his era, capable of delivering a payload of bruising checks. He played for the Stanley Cup five times, also winning with Vancouver in 1914–15, although he missed the series against Ottawa due to a broken leg.

Born in Kansas, Griffis came to hockey after his family moved to St. Catharines, Ontario, when he was 10 years old. Known for his corkscrew rushes, stalwart defensive play and knack for both dishing out and taking hits, Griffis was equally at home when the water wasn't frozen. He was a champion rower. Griffis was inducted into the Hockey Hall of Fame in 1950.

HUGH LEHMAN, GOAL

A pro since 1906 in the days of the International League, Lehman was still in action more than two decades later when he played every minute of every game for the first-year Chicago Blackhawks in the NHL, playing his final games in 1927–28 at the age of 42. Winning his first NHL game at the age of 40, Lehman set a mark that remains on the books today. He later coached the Blackhawks, becoming the first former netminder to work behind the bench of an NHL team.

Lehman played for the Stanley Cup six times, lifting it with the Millionaires in 1914–15. Nicknamed "Eagle Eye," Lehman was known for his ability to stay square to the shooter and to anticipate the play well. Always steady, and sensational when required, he was an athletic netminder capable of deflecting pucks with his hands, feet, body, legs or stick.

In the summer months, Lehman worked construction and for years served as president of his own paving company. He was inducted into the Hockey Hall of Fame in 1958.

DUNCAN (MICKEY) MACKAY, CENTRE/LEFT WING

Seeking to come west to play in the PCHA in 1914, MacKay had to beg the Patricks for a tryout, but they were certainly glad that they ultimately gave in to MacKay's persistence. It was believed out on the west coast that no one ever got around a rink faster than MacKay.

He was capable of unleashing a powerful shot while in full stride, and those who sought to try and take the stuffing out of MacKay would discover that he was also a mean cuss, willing to dish out a slash or a butt end when he was certain the referee was looking the other way.

MacKay knew he was good and didn't hesitate to share that information with the rest of the world. Skating out to the rink for the start of a game, MacKay ambled over to the net of opposition goalie Hap Holmes and pointed his stick toward a spot in the net.

"In about four minutes, Happy, I'm going down and score," MacKay informed Holmes. "And I'll shoot the puck right there." Sure enough, four minutes into the contest, MacKay beat Holmes, netting the puck in the exact spot he'd predicted.

The shifty forward played in eight Stanley Cup finals, winning with the Millionaires in 1914–15, Vancouver's only Cup winner, and with the 1928–29 Boston Bruins, the first time Boston ever won the Cup. The Hockey Hall of Fame welcomed MacKay as a member in 1952.

RAN MCDONALD, FORWARD

A speed merchant on skates, according to lore, McDonald's blazing blades once saved his life. Playing for Fort William in a road game at nearby Port Arthur in 1910, McDonald took a swing at an opponent's head with his stick. Though he missed, the local fans weren't impressed, and McDonald felt their ire the remainder of the game, but never more so than when he potted the winner in overtime. Pursued by an angry mob as he exited the ice surface, McDonald didn't look back and bolted out an arena exit, skating the two miles back to Fort William along the icy highways.

As a pro, McDonald was also well-travelled. He was the only player in PCHA history to play for all six league franchises— New Westminster, Portland, Spokane, Victoria, Seattle and Vancouver, appearing in back-to-back Stanley Cup series in 1917–18 and 1918–19.

Asked one time to list his record by a reporter, McDonald jokingly answered, "Which one? Prison or reform?"

Soon, this reference would no longer be a laughing matter. Dropped from the Seattle roster in 1920 over continued violations of training rules, McDonald's life quickly spiralled out of control. On January 15, 1920, a masked robber held up the cashier at Vancouver's Denman Arena and made off with $131 in gate receipts.

Three days later, McDonald was arrested by Vancouver police and appeared in court to answer to charges of robbery with violence.

McDonald was committed to a local sanitarium and was examined to determine if he'd suffered a nervous breakdown. He never played pro hockey again.

SINCLAIR (SPEED) MOYNES, FORWARD

As his nickname implied, Moynes was fleet of blade, one of the fastest skaters in hockey. He was also known as a clever stickhandler and a tenacious checker, capable of throwing blanket coverage over his opposite number.

During the 1918 Stanley Cup series, Moynes saw most of his duty in the two games played under the PCHA rules of seven-man hockey, subbing in as a spare when needed.

Following the 1917–18 season, Moynes enlisted in the Canadian Armed Forces and headed overseas to joining the fighting in the Great War, never to play pro hockey again. He settled in Trail, B.C. and became involved with the senior Trail Smoke Eaters, while also starting his own Pontiac dealership in the city.

RUSSELL (BARNEY) STANLEY, RIGHT WING

Stanley joined the Millionaires in their Stanley Cup winning season of 1914–15, scoring four goals in the decisive third game victory in their sweep of the Ottawa Senators.

Stanley came by his nickname as a youngster when his friends decided that Barney, the name of the family dog, suited him much better than his given name of Russell. Stanley was a straight-ahead winger with a nose for the net. "Not much use getting up and shooting the puck unless you get it on the nets," Stanley explained to the *Winnipeg Tribune*. "Clever rushes that end in the corner don't win hockey games."

Stanley was a two-time all-star in the Western Canada Hockey League and served as manager of the Chicago Blackhawks in 1927–28, suiting up for one game that season, the only NHL action of his career. At the NHL governors' meetings that season, Stanley displayed a crude prototype for a pith and fibre helmet, insisting that one day all hockey players would don headgear.

While Stanley lost to the first Toronto NHL team to win the Stanley Cup, he also maintained a connection to the most recent Toronto NHL team to win the Stanley Cup. His nephew Allan Stanley was a defenceman with the 1966–67 Maple Leafs. Barney Stanley was named to the Hockey Hall of Fame in 1962.

FRED (CYCLONE) TAYLOR, CENTRE/ROVER/DEFENCE

The Wayne Gretzky of his time, Taylor was handed his famous nickname by Canadian governor-general Earl Grey. After watching Taylor in action for the Ottawa Senators, Grey—also famous for donating the CFL's Grey Cup—was overheard to remark, "that Fred Taylor is surely a Cyclone," and the best player of the first era of pro hockey was now equipped with a nickname suitable to his talents.

A two-time Stanley Cup champion, Renfrew of the NHA paid Taylor an astonishing salary of $5,250 for a 12-game season in 1909–10, but his contemporaries were certain that he was worth every penny.

"Taylor had everything," Lester Patrick told the *Trenton Evening Times*. "He had courage, stamina, speed, stickhandling ability, the power to give a pass and accept one, the ability to score goals, and above all those things, colour, something that an outstanding athlete needs to make a manager and owner especially pleased."

The man called Cyclone was considered the greatest drawing card in hockey. "He could skate backwards as fast as the ordinary player could skate forward," Frank Patrick said. "He could shoot six ways—high or low, fast or slow, and front or back."

Taylor turned pro in the International League in 1905. He came to the PCHA in 1912 and led the league in scoring five times, including 1917–18, when he scored a league-record 32 goals. He was enshrined in the Hockey Hall of Fame in 1947.

GAME 1: MARCH 20, 1918
Toronto Hockey Club 5 Vancouver Millionaires 3

Described as a listless affair, Toronto took a lot of the stuffing out of the Millionaires by scoring three goals in the game's first 13 minutes. Reg Noble and Alf Skinner each scored twice for Toronto, while Taylor netted a pair for Vancouver.

"Noble, [Ken] Randall and [Harry] Cameron completely baffled the Vancouver team with their brilliant stickhandling," noted the *Toronto Mail and Empire*. "[Harry] Mummery broke up rush after rush and held the Vancouver forwards at his mercy."

The *Mail and Empire* offered mixed reviews after its first viewing of the Vancouver squad. "On last night's play Toronto is vastly superior but one can readily see that Cyclone Taylor would be very effective in the western style of play, which permits offsides in centre ice.

"Mickey MacKay is one of the fastest skaters that has been seen around Toronto in some time, but besides being fast is tricky and a clever stickhandler. Lloyd Cook is a very strong skater and rushes straight. He is very hard to stop, but does not seem over accurate in his shooting.

"In goal about half the Vancouver team's strength is stationed. Hugh Lehman, king of the goalkeepers on the Pacific Coast, played a wonderful game and he held the score down to the small margin presented by superlative work.

"The rest of the team are only average players and did not show anything that explained why they were in pro company."

While not as harsh in his assessment, Vancouver manager and PCHA president Frank Patrick agreed that his club was second best.

"Toronto looks like a good team," Patrick wired to his brother Lester. "Vancouver boys seemed nervous. Cook and MacKay only in form."

On the off days in between the first two games, Frank Patrick announced that George Irvine and Art Ross would referee Game 2 of the series under PCHA rules. In doing so, Ross, who started the season as player-manager of the Montreal Wanderers, would become—and remains—the only person to play in an NHL game and officiate a Stanley Cup game in the same season. NHL president Frank Calder assessed that the combination of the NHL rules and their overall weariness for a long train journey had made an impact on Vancouver's performance in Game 1, and he anticipated a better effort from the Millionaires in the second game of the set. Patrick echoed these sentiments. "Take a little tip from father," Patrick told the *Ottawa Journal*. "That old Stanley Cup is not going to leave my possession. My club is a whole lot better than they appeared in Game 1."

Toronto forward Noble suffered a shoulder injury in Game 1 and were he not able to answer the bell for Game 2, there was speculation that Toronto would be permitted to suit up Crawford in his place. Meanwhile, Vancouver defenceman Griffis announced that this would be it for him and he would retire from hockey following the Cup final series.

GAME 2: MARCH 23, 1918
Vancouver Millionaires 6 Toronto Hockey Club 4

The second game of the Stanley Cup series was described as a donnybrook. According to the *Toronto Globe* it was "a game that bristled with rough, brutal, illegal tactics, and in which good hockey apparently was the last feature considered by the players of either team." Toronto bad man Randall pulled down a pair of majors, including a slash across the arm of Taylor that put the Vancouver star out of action for the remainder of the game. Mummery laid out Moynes with an illegal check and his work was so vicious that even the Toronto fans took to booing their own player.

Vancouver grabbed a 4–1 lead late in the second period and held off a Toronto rally for the win. MacKay paced the Millionaires with a hat trick and Taylor scored twice. Skinner netted three goals for Toronto.

Judge of play Irvine was accidentally cut by Mummery's skate in the first period and while he was off for repairs, referee Ross handled the officiating duties by himself.

Ross felt that the Millionaires were in with a great opportunity to win the Cup if they were to receive favourable officiating the rest of the way. "The Blues gave a most brutal exhibition, and unless the western club gets absolute protection from the referees, they'll all be killed," Ross told the *Ottawa Journal.* Ross added that he'd fined Randall $15 for using foul and abusive language during Game 2. Toronto manager Charlie Querrie lodged a protest over the work of Irvine, and it was confirmed that Lou Marsh and Steve Vair, who officiated Game 1, would also handle Game 3.

Forget the Stanley Cup, Querrie also threw down a gauntlet to the Millionaires. "We will play Vancouver for a $1,000 side bet, half under our rules and half under western rules, provided they allow us to use Adams and Crawford and let [Stanley Cup] trustee [William] Foran of Ottawa select the referee."

GAME 3: MARCH 26, 1918

Toronto Hockey Club 6 Vancouver Millionaires 3

Back under NHL rules, Toronto raced to a 3–0 first-period lead and never looked back, getting two goals apiece from Skinner, Cameron and Corb Denneny. Taylor scored twice for Vancouver. The roughness of Game 2 was nowhere to be seen, as both teams stuck to their knitting.

Skinner was assigned the task of slowing down MacKay and he was so effective in this task that he drove the Vancouver player to distraction, MacKay spending more of his night slashing away at his check than focused on the puck.

NHL president Frank Calder felt that the two leagues needed to find common ground on a set of rules, and until they do, the outcome of the Stanley Cup series would be predictable, the title going to the team that got the extra game under its rulebook.

"Until we have uniform rules in the east and west, I don't believe there will be a really satisfactory world's series," Calder told the *Ottawa Journal*. "Toronto smothered Vancouver under eastern rules, but under the western rules, Vancouver was much the better. Play under uniform rules would be the only real test.

Calder's point was right on the money. Since the introduction of the east-west Cup final series in 1914, the team with the home-ice advantage and thus the extra game under its own rulebook had won every set.

Calder also was of the opinion that too much attention was being paid to the rough tactics of the Toronto club. "I think Toronto's rough play has been rather over-emphasized," Calder said. The only deliberate rough play has been that pulled off by Randall, and he has been well punished for it by the referees. So far as Mummery is concerned, he has used his weight, but not illegitimately. He has checked big opponents hard, but cleanly for the most part."

Calder felt that though people viewed the PCHA as more of a skating and skill league, there were plenty of players on that side of the hockey world capable of dishing out punishment.

"The Vancouver outfit is a husky crew, and the players are well able to take care of themselves," Calder said. "President Patrick, of the Ocean League, has been continually emphasizing the cleanliness of the play on the Coast and the few fights there, but it will be noticed that the only fight in the Cup series to date was started by a western player in the person of Cyclone Taylor. He pitched into [Harry] Meeking with his fists after getting a job which I thought was accidental.

"Possibly Taylor was seized with one of those freakish fits he used to show in the east when he frequently was known to toss the puck in the crowd, or do some other weird stunt."

Mummery provided the comic relief of the night when the bulky Toronto defenceman attempted a wraparound play, following the puck to the net, seeking to jam both it and Lehman into the goal. A melee ensued and concluded with all six Vancouver players piled on top of Big Mum.

Bookmakers now listed Toronto as 2–1 favourites to win the series. The Toronto club protested the utilization of PCHA official Irvine for Game 4 and he was replaced by Odie Cleghorn. Thus Cleghorn, who would make his NHL debut as a centre with the Montreal Canadiens during the 1918–19 season, and would play for the Habs in the 1919 Stanley Cup series, became the only man to officiate a game involving an NHL team before performing in the league as a player.

Calder and Frank Patrick were to meet on the off day between Games 3 and 4 to see if the two leagues couldn't hammer out a standard set of rules to govern play in both the NHL and PCHA. However, Patrick insisted little progress was made from this meeting and that it had proved brief.

"Although we had an informal conference here yesterday afternoon, President Frank Calder of the NHL and myself have not come to any understanding on uniform rules for the east and west," Patrick told the *Vancouver Daily World*, and he was critical of the NHL brand of game. "The style of hockey played here is radically different from that on the coast. Rough work predominates and is encouraged by the manager."

Patrick felt that the east should adopt the forward pass and allow kicking of the puck as was already present in the PCHA. "With six-man hockey and these improvements, the fans would see some wonderful play," Patrick said. "We find the game much speeded up in the west, and wouldn't think of going back to the old style of play."

The NHL brass believed the day of the rover was long past and wanted the west to drop the position and go with six-man hockey.

Patrick did confirm that if the Great War were to end prior to the start of the 1918–19 season, it was likely that there would be enough players out west to return a franchise to Victoria, which had been dormant the previous two seasons.

Toronto coach Dick Carroll decided that the best strategy entering Game 4 under the PCHA rulebook was to utilize his seventh player on the ice to deploy an extra defenceman and seek to clog up the middle of the defensive zone, forcing the Vancouver attackers to the perimeter.

The hope was that this would neutralize Vancouver's speed play, in which the Millionaires would throw a long pass up ice, allowing a player—usually the speedy and clever Taylor, to skate to the puck and therefore hit the defence with the puck in possession and a full head of steam, forcing the defenders to back off, creating time and space to make plays in the attacking zone.

GAME 4: MARCH 28, 1918

Vancouver Millionaires 8 Toronto Hockey Club 1

So much for strategy. Toronto was again a bunch of lost boys attempting to play under the PCHA code. Vancouver broke open a close 2–1 game early in the second period, scoring six unanswered goals over the remainder of the game. Stanley, Taylor and Lloyd Cook each scored twice for the winners.

"Torontos were simply lost at the seven-game game," the *Toronto Globe* reported. "Vancouver ran all over them with speed and had a bag of tricks that left the Blue Shirts gasping.

"Toronto tried the three-man defence play, but it didn't bother the Westerners. They streaked in two, three and four at a time, and Holmes was simply helpless before the onslaught."

This would be just the second Stanley Cup series to go the full five-game limit. The Montreal Canadiens and Portland Rosebuds need five games to decide the title that spring, the Habs taking a 2–1 decision in the final match under NHL rules to win the Cup for the first time in franchise history.

There was plenty of bad blood as the decisive fifth game of the Stanley Cup series approached. Both Vancouver's Stanley and Toronto's Randall were forced to leave Game 4 after absorbing punishing hits and there was talk of retribution.

"Manager Charlie Querrie of the Torontos threatens to get us on Saturday night," Vancouver coach Patrick told the *Vancouver Daily World*, going as far as to hint there was a criminal element present among the Toronto roster. "Some of the Toronto players may land in gaol if they start anything."

On the eve of Game 5, both teams got into a heated debate over who would officiate the tilt. "Frank Patrick wired me today to state that the clubs were unable to agree, and requested me to appoint the referees," Stanley Cup trustee William Foran told the *Montreal Gazette*.

Foran named Harvey Pulford of Ottawa and Russell Bowie of Montreal, both of them Stanley Cup winners in their playing days, to handle the whistles. Tom Melville was Foran's first choice, but when Melville was unavailable, Bowie reluctantly agreed to take his place.

"I feel that in getting Pulford and Bowie I have secured the best men available," Foran said. "These officials know the rules thoroughly, and will not hesitate to enforce them to the letter.

"Neither wishes to act, and I had trouble inducing them to do so. I have instructed Mr. Pulford and Mr. Bowie to be very strict with regard to rough play, and to punish most severely any players who violate the rules and rough it unnecessarily. Their instructions, in fact, are to keep the game clean at any cost."

GAME 5: MARCH 30, 1918
Toronto Hockey Club 2 Vancouver Millionaires 1

The tightest contest of the series saw the teams battle through two scoreless periods. A minute into the third period, Toronto forward Skinner zipped a high hard one that found the upper corner of the net behind Lehman to open the scoring.

At that point, the tight checking, defensive struggle ceased and the game opened up to a terrific pace. Pressuring the Toronto defence with persistent forechecking, Vancouver grabbed the equalizer. MacKay intercepted a Toronto clearance attempt, stickhandled his way toward the net and whipped a pass to Taylor on the edge of the Toronto net, and the cagey veteran batted it home to tie the game.

A hero was needed, and one would step forward. Diminutive Toronto forward Corb Denneny carried the puck toward the Vancouver defence with pace. As they closed down on him, Denneny lunged sharply and split his way between the pairing, pushing the puck past them to open ice.

Careening through the opening on one skate, Denneny was able to gather up the puck and scoop it past Lehman, his momentum carrying him crashing into the goalpost a split second after his tally.

There were still nine minutes to play, but Toronto held its lead this time and the Stanley Cup belonged to the team from the Queen City.

"Toronto undoubtedly is the best team," the *Vancouver Daily World* acknowledged. "That has been evident throughout the series, but the Vancouver team improved in every game and played their best on Saturday night."

Adding to their loss there was another sour note for the Millionaires. Sub forward Ran McDonald evidently ran afoul of team discipline on the eve of the most important game of the season.

"McDonald, who made such a good impression in the first four games, was worse than useless to his team Saturday," the *Vancouver Daily World* noted. "It was reported that just before the game he was fined $50 for breaking training rules."

Holmes and Cameron of the Toronto club had also won the 1913–14 Stanley Cup with the NHA Toronto Blue Shirts. Meanwhile, Holmes was a back-to-back Cup winner, triumphing with the PCHA's Seattle Metropolitans in 1916–17.

The series was a financial success—crowds were between 5,500 and 6,000 for each game. The winning Toronto players each received a prize of $350 as their share of the gate receipts, while each member of the losing Millionaires pocketed $250. But the antics off the ice displayed that pro hockey still had a long journey ahead before it could be classified as a major league sport.

The different code of rules between the leagues made the Stanley Cup series somewhat of a farce. The NHL team won every game under its rules and the PCHA club won easily playing twice by their rulebook. The unnecessary rough play was also panned by critics. It didn't help the optics from the outside that one of the league presidents—Frank Patrick of the PCHA—was also coaching one of the teams in the Cup final set.

"The whole series was certainly a haphazard affair," the *Ottawa Journal* reported. "Nobody seemed to know just who was in charge of affairs or who was the real boss. Frank Patrick and his Vancouver team arrived in Toronto to play the blues two weeks ago, and the western magnate professed himself ignorant of arrangements."

There was also the issue of the teams having too much say in the appointment of referees for the Stanley Cup games, a factor that only served to further taint the series. "Whether players like an official or not is something that should not be considered when the officers of the league are satisfied that he is honest and competent," noted the *Ottawa Journal*. "In a series like the Stanley Cup, the two best officials in the rival leagues should have been selected to act and sentry right down the line through the series.

"That is the only fair and satisfactory way. This dickering about officials is picayune, and only cheapens teams, clubs, leagues and officials, and makes the sporting public sick of the whole thing. It was bush league stuff in what should have been a big league series."

Patrick blasted away at the set-up in Toronto for the series, insisting it was intimidating to his players. "The gambling and police interference with visiting players are very bad features in Toronto," Patrick told the *Ottawa Journal*. "The public will immediately lose confidence in the game when it becomes known that the gamblers are in close touch with the players.

"We would not tolerate anything of the kind in the west, and I don't think it would be allowed to run in any other eastern city."

Patrick also pointed out that his team was forced to deal with the high-handed tactics of the constabulary stationed at the games, a charge that was also levied during the NHL season by Montreal Canadiens manager George Kennedy.

"We were warned by police that immediate arrest would follow any rough play, but no steps were taken when the Toronto players cut us up," Patrick complained.

He also fired a shot at the Toronto media. "The gambling-police-newspaper combination will not improve the game any there," Patrick said. "The newspapers are not inclined to give a visiting team any credit for winning a game, but roast the home team when it loses for being off colour."

Patrick also wondered aloud that if the war continued in Europe, would the pro hockey season even be permitted to exist for the 1918–19 campaign?

TROPHY CASE
Conn Smythe Trophy
Winner: Alf Skinner, Toronto Hockey Club

The Toronto forward figured in at least one goal in every game of the series, sharing the goal-scoring lead in the series with eight in five games. He tallied a hat trick, including the game winner, in Toronto's Game 1 verdict. He netted two goals apiece in Games 2 and 3 and set up Toronto's only goal in Game 4. In Toronto's decisive Game 5 triumph, Skinner opened the scoring.

Runner-Up: Fred (Cyclone) Taylor, Vancouver Millionaires

The veteran campaigner and 1917–18 PCHA scoring champion netted a goal in all five games of the series. He tallied at least twice in each of the first four games, and it was Taylor's goal that pulled Vancouver even in the third period of Game 5. Four of his goals either tied the game or gave the Millionaires the lead.

THE ROAD AHEAD

The NHL had survived its inaugural season—barely—but the one-year experiment was still a long way from becoming a century-old juggernaut. When Eddie Livingstone, the former owner of the Toronto franchise, tried to throw a monkey wrench into the plans of Canada's pro hockey moguls by attempting to reorganize the NHA, the other owners simply carried on with NHL.

"This is the most important hockey league meeting ever held in Canada," was how NHL president Frank Calder characterized the November 9, 1918 gathering in Montreal that officially christened the league going forward as the NHL.

A five-year agreement was signed by the owners of the four clubs. "The five-year agreement between the clubs is very important," Calder told the *Ottawa Journal*. "It will prevent the possibility of the repetition of the squabble such as we had this fall."

Canadiens owner George Kennedy couldn't resist getting in another dig at his old nemesis. "Livingstone has made us a real league," Kennedy said. "We were more or less disjointed but now we are solid.

"We owe Livingstone a vote of thanks for what he has done for us. He has created a lot of newspaper ink as well, which will not do any harm."

"Livingstone helped to make the NHL a real league out of the shaky proposition," Calder added.

Not everyone associated with the NHL viewed Livingstone as a cancerous tumour. "He was a great man for ideas," suggested Ottawa Senators forward Cy Denneny, who played for Livingstone's Toronto team in the NHA. Among those good ideas, Livingstone was given credit as the first coach to alternate set forward lines, rather than sub in for individual players as they grew tired. The split schedule and post-season league playoff were also Livingstone's ideas.

"One thing Livingstone did in a way no other owner before or since has equalled was to uncover new talent," the *Ottawa Journal* noted. "What other owner can show a list like [Duke] Keats, [Archie] Briden, the two Dennenys [Corb and Cy], [Alf] Skinner, [Reg] Noble, [Harry] Meeking and [Jack] Brown? All unearthed from the bushes by the astute Edward?"

Percy Quinn of Toronto, manager of the Arena Gardens, who had acquired an option on purchasing the dormant Quebec franchise, was not present at the NHL meeting, and a telegram was sent to him and he was given until 6:00 p.m. November 11, 1918 to state his intentions for his franchise.

Quinn requested permission to move the Quebec club to play as a second team in Toronto, and when this was denied by the NHL governors, he allowed his option on the club to expire.

Ted Dey, owner of the Ottawa arena, revealed that on October 2, 1918, he had accepted a $15 down payment from an unnamed Toronto man to gain an option on the rink for a rival pro league, an option that had a 30-day window and had expired without being acted upon. Dey then announced that the Ottawa Senators had since been granted exclusive pro privileges to his arena for the upcoming season.

It was later discovered that the league in search of ice time in Canada's capital city was in fact the CHA, and that the man who gained the option was Quinn. In partnership with Livingstone, the two men proposed that their rival loop would consist of teams in Montreal, Quebec, Ottawa and Toronto, and that he'd approached top players such as Newsy Lalonde, Odie Cleghorn and Frank Foyston to join his league.

The owners of the Toronto Arena Company were queried as to whether they had been approached by the CHA. "None whatsoever," Arena manager Charlie Querrie said, who also couldn't stop himself from adding a sarcastic flourish.

"Telegrams only cost 25 cents each."

There was good news on the international front. The end of the Great War on November 11, 1918, resulted in the return of players who'd served their country in battle returning to the ice. The Montreal Canadiens added Amos Arbour and Fred Doherty, and Harry (Punch) Broadbent returned to Ottawa, wearing the Military Medal for his service on the battlefield.

Just three teams would answer the bell as the NHL's second campaign got underway—the Montreal Canadiens, Toronto Arenas and Ottawa Senators. Quebec opted to take another year off from competition, and before the season was out, the Stanley Cup champion Arenas—as they'd finally been officially christened by the club's ownership group—would also take a hike.

There were strange goings-on in Toronto all season long in 1918–19. Two games into the campaign, the Seattle

The end of the war.

Metropolitans of the PCHA recalled goalie Harry (Hap) Holmes from his loan to the Arenas. In mid-January, defenceman Harry Cameron and forward Reg Noble were dropped from the team for disciplinary reasons.

"Reg Noble and Harry Cameron, two members of the Arena pros, have been suspended without pay by the management of the local team," the *Toronto World* reported. "The reason is failure to live up to training rules." This terminology was often used as code to disguise their real offense, which was drinking and carousing too frequently

"These two players have been in trouble for this reason before and the management has decided that it is time to call a halt."

Less than a week later, Cameron, rumoured to be one of the highest-paid players in the NHL, was loaned to Ottawa for the remainder of the season.

Money remained a big issue within the league. Speculation was that Cameron pocketed $900 a season. Paul Jacobs, the first Native Canadian to play in the NHL, quit Toronto after one game because he'd landed a job in Montreal. Joe Malone, the NHL scoring champion in 1917–18, who potted a league-leading 44 goals, played just eight games for the Canadiens in 1918–19, scoring seven goals. He was working in a bank in Quebec City and couldn't get the time off work to travel to Montreal for most games, and road trips were out of the question.

"I had hooked onto a good job in Quebec City which promised a secure future, something in those days hockey couldn't," Malone told author Andy O'Brien in his book *Fire-Wagon Hockey*.

Without Cameron, the NHL's best defenceman, Toronto just kept losing. The Arenas went 3–9 to open the season, and in February, first Harry Meeking and then Ken Randall were also let go by the team, both heading east to play in Glace Bay, Nova Scotia.

Following a 9–3 loss to the Senators in Ottawa on February 20, 1919, a result that clinched the second-half regular-season title for Ottawa, Toronto players Harry Mummery and Rusty Crawford shook hands with the Ottawa players and said,

"Good-bye until next season." Arenas coach Dick Carroll confirmed after the game that the team was done for the year.

The next day it was made official that the reigning Stanley Cup champions had folded. "I have been notified by telephone by [Toronto] manager [Charlie] Querrie that the Arena club was through, and that their remaining two games away and at home would be defaulted," Calder told the *Toronto World*.

To make up for the lost dates, Calder hastily organized a best-of-seven playoff for the NHL title between the Senators and Montreal Canadiens, the first-half champions.

While the Toronto situation was alarming, the opportunity for future NHL growth elsewhere appeared to be increasing. Quebec was reported to be finally ready to ice a team in time for the 1919–20 season and Hamilton, where a new arena was being constructed, also expressed interest in acquiring a franchise.

Off the ice, there were other problems which needed to be addressed. Rejected in 1917, his original lawsuit thrown out of court in the late winter of 1918 and his attempt to give rebirth to the NHA scuttled in the fall of the year, the NHL was discovering that Livingstone was nothing if he wasn't persistent. He wasn't going to go away without putting up a fight.

Livingstone wouldn't give up on the idea of launching a rival league in the CHA. He had recruited Quinn, owner of the 1913–14 Stanley Cup champion Toronto Blueshirts as his partner, and together they set out seeking homes for franchises in their proposed league.

They immediately ran into roadblocks. Since the majority of NHL clubs were owned by the arena companies in each city, the chance of finding suitable ice time in NHL towns was almost non-existent, so Quinn and Livingstone decided to do what they did best—they filed lawsuits.

In January of 1919, Quinn filed suit against Dey, the Ottawa Arena and Tommy Gorman of the Senators for $10,000, arguing that the two men had conspired to renege on a promise to allow a CHA team to play in the facility. But much like Livingstone's suit against the NHL, Quinn was a loser when he had his day in court and his lawsuit was tossed.

The Canadiens won the NHL title and headed west to face the Metropolitans in a rematch of the 1916–17 Stanley Cup final, but tragedy would ensure that there would be no winner.

The Spanish influenza epidemic was at the time sweeping across the globe, infecting an estimated 500 million people and killing between 50–100 million, and hockey would not go unscathed. Already, former Senators defenceman Hamby Shore's life had been claimed in October of 1918, and as the Habs headed toward Seattle, the virus was waiting to engulf them.

Following an especially taxing double-overtime game that was eventually called as a scoreless tie, the Seattle fans were of the opinion that Canadiens defenceman (Bad) Joe Hall came by his nicknamed deservedly. He'd utilized his stick to carve up the face of Seattle forward Jack Walker during the game.

"His methods are of the slashing, reckless bodychecking variety and he can bear a lot of watching tomorrow," the *Seattle Daily Times* reported. "The attitude of the fans toward this sort of work was shown in the hoots and hisses which followed his rushes down the ice."

Though none of those catcalling Seattle spectators could possibly know it, Hall was rapidly running out of tomorrows.

Montreal won the next game 4–3 to pull even in the series, but then several of the Canadiens players fell ill and the decisive fifth game required postponement.

So many Canadiens were struck down with influenza that Montreal could suit up just three healthy skaters. "The sickest men are Jack McDonald and Joe Hall, who are very sick indeed, each of them with a fever of 104," reported the *Seattle Daily Times*. "Slightly ill are Newsy Lalonde, Louis Berlinquette and [Billy] Coutu and manager George Kennedy.

"The final decision as to calling off the series has been postponed for 24 hours while doctors watch the cases of Lalonde, Berlinquette and Coutu to see how they hold up."

It was believed that the Canadiens players might have contracted the disease while in Victoria, B.C., en route to Seattle. Seven of the players on Victoria's PCHA club were bedridden with flu earlier in the season.

There was talk of utilizing some of those Victoria players to fill out the Canadiens roster and finish the series, but it was instead decided to call off the Cup final. Seattle was offered the trophy by default but declined.

Within days, Metropolitans defenceman Roy Rickey and manager Pete Muldoon were also hospitalized with flu. In the meantime, most of the Canadiens were rallying.

"Joe Hall is the only one who is not pronounced out of danger," the *Seattle Daily Times* reported on April 4, 1919. He was quarantined at the Seattle Sanitarium. "Hall has a mighty serious case of pneumonia, so serious that his mother Emily Hall left Vancouver for Seattle to attend her son personally."

The next day, Hall was dead at the age of 37.

"Joe Hall was one of the real veterans of hockey," PCHA president Frank Patrick told the *Montreal Gazette*. "He had been playing senior hockey since 1902.

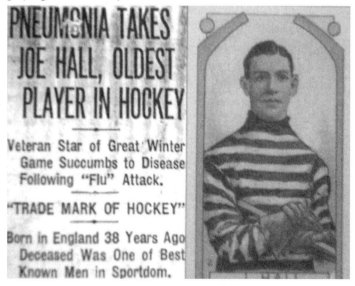

PNEUMONIA TAKES JOE HALL, OLDEST PLAYER IN HOCKEY

Veteran Star of Great Winter Game Succumbs to Disease Following "Flu" Attack.

"TRADE MARK OF HOCKEY"

Born in England 38 Years Ago Deceased Was One of Best Known Men in Sportdom.

"The game suffered a loss by his passing. Off the ice, he was one of the jolliest, best hearted, most popular men who ever played."

Hall's Montreal teammates accompanied his body back to his final resting place in his home of Brandon, Manitoba.

The league needed reorganizing again in the fall of 1919 and with only two viable teams, for a time there was speculation that the NHL might suspend operations. At the league's annual meeting on November 23, 1919, it was announced that the NHL would indeed operate for the 1919–20 season and would in fact be a four-team outfit for the first time since the launch of the league in 1917.

Quebec was finally going to ice a team. Mike Quinn would manage the club and all the players whose rights belonged to the team would be returned to the fold, including McDonald, Malone and Mummery.

On November 26, 1919, Fred Hambly, who was head of the Toronto Board of Education, headed a group that purchased the dormant Toronto NHL franchise and rechristened it the Tecumsehs, the nickname by which one of Toronto's two NHA franchises had gone in 1912–13. But after a week of sober thought, Hambly changed his mind, decided he'd prefer to have the luck of the Irish on his side and announced that the team would be called the St. Patricks.

In early January, 1920, Livingstone finally won his battle with the NHL. He was awarded $20,000 in a lawsuit he'd launched against the Toronto Arena Company. Livingstone insisted they had not paid him for the players he had under contract prior to the birth of the NHL and the court agreed with him. But his bid to gain control of the rink, which would have guaranteed that he could have put a CHA team in Toronto, failed to materialize when the court ruled that the receiver would continue to operate the facility.

Quebec endured one forgettable 4–20 season, the only highlight being Malone's seven-goal performance on January

31, 1920 that set an NHL single-game mark that remains on the books today. But by the end of the season, it was clear that Quebec was in over its head as an NHL franchise. The team drew less than 1,000 fans at the box office each game, it proved to be a terrible road draw, and the other three NHL teams were growing weary of the long train trip up to Quebec City to play.

On November 2, 1920, the NHL announced that the Quebec franchise would be relocated to Hamilton and that the franchise, to be known as the Tigers, would be purchased by Percy Thompson, owner of the arena in Hamilton.

The reason why the league opted to go to Hamilton was twofold. They needed somewhere to put the Quebec club, and what better place than one of the cities that Livingstone and Percy Quinn were eyeing in their never-ending quest to get the CHA off the ground? The league also needed a backup home for the St. Patricks, because Mutual Street Arena in Toronto had gone into receivership due to the legal costs the rink's owners had incurred in their fight with Livingstone, and its immediate future was uncertain.

Thompson indicated he was scared off from the CHA by Livingstone's proclamation that player salaries in his league would run between $1,800-$2,000 per player. At the time, the NHL sought to stay loyal to a soft salary cap of $5,000 per team.

By December of 1920, it became clear that the Toronto General Trust would operate the rink in the city, and the St. Patricks would remain in Toronto. What was unclear was whether the receivers would also allot ice time to a team from Livingstone's proposed league.

"The idea of the receivers is to get every nickel possible out of the arena, and if the CHA would be willing to carry on and pay the rental asked, there is not a shadow of a doubt but that the receivers would take them in," the *Ottawa Journal* reported.

Livingstone boldly claimed that he had deals with players such as Newsy Lalonde, Bert Corbeau and Amos Arbour of the Canadiens, Sprague Cleghorn of Ottawa, Toronto's Cully

Wilson, Hamilton's Goldie Prodger and amateur Ernie Parkes. One by one, all of these players inked pacts with the NHL teams, while Parkes announced he would retain his amateur standing, causing the *Ottawa Journal* to call the new loop the "Quinn-Livingstone Hot-Air Bureau" and the "Mythical Hockey League.

"Whoever dubbed the Quinn-Livingstone outfit a league of lies didn't under estimate their case."

No one within the NHL's inner circle was going to let their feud with Livingstone die. Even the Canadiens' owner Kennedy, on his deathbed in the fall of 1921, was still was taking shots at Livingstone. With several of the NHL owners gathered at his side to say their final goodbyes, Kennedy scanned the room and joked, "Did you bring Eddie Livingstone up, too?"

Livingstone was back in court again in October of 1923 and looked to be a big winner when a Toronto court awarded him $100,000 in damages, insisting the league and the Toronto Arena Company had not properly compensated him for the loss of his team and his players. But on appeal, Livingstone's award was reduced to $10,000. A month later, his rival league dream was again in the news, as he and Quinn announced plans to construct a new arena in Montreal. There was a slight glitch in his plans however: Livingstone didn't have the financial backing in place to begin construction.

Livingstone also launched a magazine titled *Sport and Bowler*, in which he frequently penned articles critical of the NHL.

In February of 1924, Livingstone opted to take a different tack, applying for an NHL expansion franchise. He claimed at this time to the NHL officials that he had no involvement in any proposed new league. Meanwhile, Montreal racetrack operator Tom Duggan and grocery store magnate C.F. Adams of Boston met with the NHL owners to discuss international expansion to American cities, including New York and Boston.

The NHL opted for expansion in the fall of 1924, adding a second team in Montreal, called the Maroons, to be owned by James Strachan and to be managed by Cecil Hart, publicity director for the Montreal Wanderers during their brief NHL tenure in 1917–18. The league also went south of the border for the first time, granting Adams a franchise, the Boston Bruins. As his manager, Adams hired former Wanderers player-manager and original NHLer Art Ross. Once again, Livingstone was left out in the cold.

The story of the 1924–25 NHL season would belong to the Hamilton Tigers. After four successive last-place finishes, they raced to the top of the league and stayed there, finishing first overall.

It was then that the trouble began. The NHL schedule had expanded from 24 to 30 games that season with the addition of the Maroons and the Bruins to the fold. While several teams bumped up the salaries of their players following this development, Hamilton management did not, and this didn't sit too well with players, who insisted that they'd been promised a $200 bonus per player.

Led by captain Shorty Green and goaltender Jake Forbes— the latter who had sat out the entire 1921–22 season in a contract dispute with Toronto, his original NHL team—the Tigers walked off the job, demanding their $200 bonus. Otherwise they would not play in the NHL final.

"The boys are unanimous in what they consider their just dues, hence the reason for the stand we have taken," Green said. Ownership offered each player $100 but they wouldn't budge from their original demand.

Calder wasn't about to stand for this insubordination and suspended each of the Hamilton players indefinitely, rubbing salt in the wound by adding a $200 fine to each player.

"The players of the Hamilton club, having refused to complete their contracts unless they received additional payment, the club is declared in default," Calder said in a statement.

After originally threatening to insert fourth-place Ottawa into the playoffs in place of the Tigers, Calder opted to send the winner of the Toronto-Canadiens semi-final out west to represent the NHL in the Stanley Cup final.

"I would like to point out," Calder continued, "that the league will lose close to $8,000 from Hamilton's action. This money would have been taken in at the two games between Canadiens and Hamilton. By payment of $2,000 to Hamilton, the amount asked by the [10] players, we could have carried on the series and taken in that $8,000.

"It can thus be seen that we are paying dearly from a money end for our action, but we are willing to take it to make an example of the Hamilton players and a warning for all future time."

There wouldn't be another labour dispute in the NHL until the 1992 players' strike.

Boston owner Adams described the Hamilton strike as, "one of the worst crises in the history of the game. Furthermore, they ruined the game as far as Hamilton is concerned," Adams told the *Ottawa Journal*. "Pro hockey is done in that city."

Originally, the Hamilton owners insisted that they would be back for the 1925–26 NHL season with an entirely new lineup of players.

"As a matter of fact," Andrew Ross, one of four owners of the Hamilton team told the *Montreal Gazette*, "we have had an offer already from a club in the league for the players and it is our intention to sell them."

Well, that wasn't quite true. Yes, there had been an offer for the entire Hamilton roster, although it wasn't coming from an existing NHL team but rather a team that would soon exist.

Thompson, owner of the Hamilton's Barton Street Arena and majority owner of the Tigers, was already in conversation with Tex Rickard, the legendary New York boxing promoter, about selling his team to New York interests. Rickard needed to book dates at Madison Square Garden and felt hockey was a sport that could fill the bill.

Following the Hamilton strike, who showed up again and started talk of a rival league? You guessed it—the NHL's old foe

Livingstone was at it once more, meeting with Gorman—the same person his partner Quinn had sued six years earlier—and Lalonde to discuss the possibility of developing an entity to compete with the NHL. Cities associated with this potential new pro league included Toronto, Ottawa, Montreal, Boston, Pittsburgh, Windsor and Cleveland. Livingstone even talked of building a rink in Detroit.

Some felt that in its shortsightedness over the Hamilton issue, the NHL was opening the door to a rival league. "If the NHL owners had shown more of an inclination to cater to the fans rather than the box office end of the game, pro hockey could have been put on a sound foundation and the fans would have been more loyal," was the opinion of the *Detroit Free Press*. "The recent fiasco which terminated the playoff series of the past season did a great deal of harm. If it did nothing else, it created a suspicion in the minds of the game's adherents that all was not right in the organization and that the Hamilton players were probably more justified in their action than appeared on the surface.

"Not so many years ago, pro league hockey in Canada reeked with scandals and the fans passed it up in favour of the OHA hockey or senior amateur games. During the past two or three years, the NHL has steadily overcome this feeling concerning the pros and gradually converted many fans."

There was speculation that the suspended Hamilton players, as well as the Stanley Cup champion Victoria Cougars, had been contacted by the group seeking to launch the proposed new league. Lalonde was expected to operate the Montreal club and felt confident he could convince Canadiens stars Aurel Joliat and Billy Boucher to jump ship.

"A hockey war would be a lively one and would affect the amateurs as well as the present pro clubs," the *Detroit Free Press* predicted. "Hockey salaries have been increasing every season, but keen competition for players would put the latter in the position where they will be almost able to name their own terms.

"After it is all over, pro hockey will either be down and out, or in a better organized state than ever before."

While the Hamilton mess was unfolding, Duggan, Rickard, and Madison Square Garden president Col. John T. Hammond announced they had come to an agreement on an exclusive contract for the new NHL team to play at the Garden. Gorman signed a five-year contract as manager of the team and was given an interest in ownership of the club as well.

Rickard, the man who bankrolled promotions of such legendary pugilists as Jack Johnson, Jack Dempsey and Gene Tunney, felt the NHL was well capable of punching above its weight class.

"I can make bigger money with less worry and fewer risks out of hockey than I have been getting out of boxing," Rickard said.

Curiously, Duggan and Gorman, and Boston's Adams, who'd all been involved with Livingstone in the past in talks regarding the proposed International League to rival the NHL, were all now situated under the NHL umbrella, while Livingstone found himself situated in his usual place—on the outside looking in.

On September 26, 1925, the entire Hamilton roster was sold to the new club in New York—to be called the Americans—for $75,000. Every player was reinstated from suspension after paying their $200 fines.

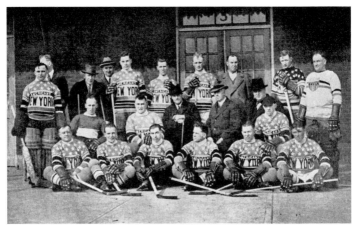

The New York Americans.

The small-market Hamilton club had likely been living on borrowed time, regardless of the player strike. The NHL was growing rapidly into a major-league sporting entity. Ottawa, a powerhouse club during the NHL's first decade, would also soon find it impossible to compete.

Unable to join them, Livingstone decided to try to beat them again. The NHL found itself back in a courtroom with Livingstone in the fall of 1925, hearing another appeal of his breach of contract suit against the Toronto Hockey Club and the Arena Gardens, taking his case to the highest court in the British Empire, the London, England-based Judicial Committee of the Privy Council. He was seeking to get his original $100,000 award reinstated.

Livingstone's lawyer W.N. Tilley told the court that under a 1917 agreement, the contracts for the players on Livingstone's Toronto NHA club were to be turned over to the Arena Gardens, to be held in trust. Tilley argued that a deliberate scheme had been entered into to deprive Livingstone of these players. He said that when the 1918–19 season opened, "a new partnership was started whereby [Arena manager] Hubert Vearncombe said, 'I'm carrying on,' and he made contracts with the players for the season of 1918–19, and then sold the team to a syndicate known as St. Patricks [in 1919] and it has been operated under that name ever since."

A.C. McMaster, representing the Arena Gardens, indicated that his clients were willing to raise the damages awarded to Livingstone to $12,000 if it would bring about the end of the litigation. Instead, in their ruling on July 27, 1926, the court dismissed the appeal without costs, deciding that without players or a franchise, it was an impossible task to put a dollar amount on what Livingstone was owed.

More changes were afoot in the league. The Pittsburgh Pirates were added as an NHL expansion team for the 1925–26 season and made history, qualifying for the playoffs to become the first American-based NHL team to enter post-season play.

Despite the best efforts of the NHL brass, Livingstone wasn't about to let his dream of a rival league die. In New York in February of 1926 he announced the latest plans for his International Professional Hockey League, installing himself as league president. The new circuit, Livingstone claimed, would count franchises in Chicago, Toronto, Detroit and Buffalo, as well as two teams in New York.

"Notification will be given the star hockey players throughout the United States and Canada to be ready to consider contracts in the near future," Livingstone told *Associated Press*. "The signing of players will begin within the next 60 days, when the few remaining franchises will have been allotted." Articles of incorporation for the league were filed with the Michigan Secretary of State in April of 1926 and the company was capitalized at $110,000.

It was certainly a good time to play hockey for a living. The excess of the 1920s was also finding its way to the ice rink. Salaries were exploding around the NHL, as top amateurs commanded big bucks to turn pro. Toronto paid Clarence (Hap) Day $5,000 a season to get his name on a pro pact. Pittsburgh coughed up $7,500 to Lionel Conacher, and the Maroons signed Dunc Munro, captain of Canada's 1924 Olympic gold medal winner, for $7,000.

The value of an NHL franchise had also increased exponentially. In 1921, Leo Dandurand had acquired the Canadiens for $11,000. In 1925, he insured the club for $150,000.

The NHL was now big-time, and it was about to get bigger. Following the 1925–26 season, the Western Hockey League, which had succeeded the PCHA as the NHL's top rival in 1924 when the PCHA and Western Canada Hockey League merged, folded up operations and the Patrick brothers began selling off the contracts of its players to NHL clubs.

With all this excess hockey talent now on the market, there was no reason to prevent another NHL growth spurt. Three new teams were added, bringing the league up to a 10-team loop. The

Detroit Cougars, New York Rangers and Chicago Blackhawks were the new clubs that came aboard in time for the 1926–27 season, and the NHL divided into two five-team divisions for the first time.

"In the larger American cities, they are prepared to pay higher prices," expressed Lloyd Turner, owner of the WHL's Calgary Tigers. "It is a situation I felt would arise as soon as the United States cities took up hockey."

At the same time, NHL nemesis Livingstone was finally a franchise owner in a league. He was the money behind the Chicago Cardinals of the minor-pro American Hockey Association, which launched play in 1926–27. But if he thought he was safe from persecution by the NHL, Livingstone was sadly mistaken. Viewing the inclusion of Livingstone and the placing of his team in Chicago in direct competition with the NHL Blackhawks, Calder immediately ruled the AHA to be an outlaw league and ended any working agreement between the NHL and AHA. Making things even more tense, both the Blackhawks and Cardinals played out of the same rink, the Chicago Coliseum.

Since the NHL declined to honour AHA contracts, the Blackhawks raided the Cardinals roster, signing Cy Wentworth, Ted Graham, Bobby Burns and Ralph Taylor to NHL deals. The AHA was pressured by Calder and the NHL moguls to remove Livingstone.

Livingstone denied that he was suing the league, arguing that his legal troubles were with Toronto's Arena Gardens group, and not with the NHL. "I haven't started any suit whatever and have no knowledge of any suit being filed by any other member of our organization," Livingstone insisted to the *Chicago Tribune*.

The problems would be solved if Livingstone sold the team, the *Winnipeg Tribune* reported. "President Calder has no axe to grind with our league," the *Tribune* wrote. "But apparently, he and the NHL have an axe to grind with Livingstone.

"The dope is that if Mr. Livingstone disposes of his interests in the Chicago club, then all will be smooth sailing once more."

Eventually, Livingstone gave up the battle and sold his franchise to Chicago interests on March 8, 1927, but he was far from done fighting.

On December 23, 1927, Livingstone filed a $700,000 lawsuit in U.S. Federal Court, alleging that Calder, AHA president Alvin H. Warren and Blackhawks owner Major Frederic McLaughlin had conspired to put his Chicago franchise out of business and drive him from the game.

The case finally went to court in 1930, but was twice declared a mistrial—once because a juror was found to have conversed with McLaughlin, and the other time after a motion filed by Livingstone's lawyer Cecil C. Erickson, who was dissatisfied with the fragmentary methods in which evidence was presented. The motion was granted. The suit was never refiled and eventually dismissed.

Four years earlier, Livingstone's legal battles with the NHL over his Toronto franchise concluded with him a winner. He was awarded a $15,000 settlement—$10,000 for the loss of his team and $5,000 for estimated lost profits.

After the conclusion of his failed Chicago lawsuit, Livingstone faded from the pro hockey scene, returning to amateur hockey, working with the OHA and coaching the Toronto Young Lions. He died in 1945.

The NHL endured some hard times during the Great Depression, eventually being reduced to a six-team outfit in 1942. But the league blossomed following World War II into a powerful outfit, and starting with a six-team expansion in 1967, began a consistently upward motion that would see it become a 31-team league with the addition of the Las Vegas Golden Knights for the 2017–18 season.

And when you think about it, they've all got Eddie Livingstone to thank for it.

APPENDIX 1
THE SEASON THAT WAS

NHL First Half Scores

	GWG
Dec. 19, 1917	
Toronto Hockey Club 9 at Montreal Wanderers 10	Dave Ritchie
Montreal Canadiens 7 at Ottawa Senators 4	Joe Malone
Dec. 22, 1917	
Montreal Wanderers 2 at Montreal Canadiens 11	Didier Pitre
Ottawa Senators 4 at Toronto Hockey Club 11	Reg Noble
Dec. 26, 1917	
Ottawa Senators 6 at Montreal Wanderers 3	Jack Darragh
Montreal Canadiens 5 at Toronto Hockey Club 7	Harry Cameron
Dec. 29, 1917	
Montreal Wanderers 2 at Ottawa Senators 9	Cy Denneny
Toronto Hockey Club 2 at Montreal Canadiens 9	Didier Pitre
Jan. 2, 1918	
Toronto Hockey Club 6 at Ottawa Senators 5	Reg Noble
Montreal Canadiens 1 Montreal Wanderers 0	(Forfeit)
Jan. 5, 1918	
Ottawa Senators 5 at Montreal Canadiens 6 (OT)	Joe Malone
Toronto Hockey Club 1 Montreal Wanderers 0	(Forfeit)

Jan. 9, 1918
Montreal Canadiens 4 at Toronto Hockey Club 6   Reg Noble

Jan. 12, 1918
Ottawa Senators 4 at Montreal Canadiens 9   Joe Malone

Jan. 14, 1918
Toronto Hockey Club 6 at Ottawa Senators 9   Harry Hyland

Jan. 16, 1918
Ottawa Senators 4 at Toronto Hockey Club 5   Ken Randall

Jan. 19, 1918
Toronto Hockey Club 1 at Montreal Canadiens 5   Didier Pitre

Jan. 21, 1918
Montreal Canadiens 5 at Ottawa Senators 3   Joe Hall

Jan. 23, 1918
Ottawa Senators 4 at Montreal Canadiens 3   Harry Hyland

Jan. 26, 1918
Toronto Hockey Club 3 at Ottawa Senators 6   Cy Denneny

Jan. 28. 1918
Montreal Canadiens 1 at Toronto Hockey Club 5   Ken Randall

Jan. 30, 1918
Montreal Canadiens 5 at Ottawa Senators 2   Joe Malone

Feb. 2, 1918
Toronto Hockey Club 2 at Montreal Canadiens 11   Didier Pitre

Feb. 4, 1918
Ottawa Senators 2 at Toronto Hockey Club 8   Harry Mummery

Appendix 1

NHL First Half Standings

TEAM	GP	W	L	F	A	P	H	A	OT
Montreal Canadiens-x	14	10	4	81	47	20	5–1	4–3	1–0
Toronto Hockey Club	14	8	6	71	75	16	6–0	1–6	0–0
Ottawa Senators	14	5	9	67	79	10	3–4	2–5	0–1
Montreal Wanderers-y	6	1	5	17	35	2	1–1	0–2	0–0

x-Canadiens clinched spot in NHL playoffs.

y-Wanderers dropped out of league after their rink burnt down on Jan. 2, 1918. Toronto and Canadiens each won one game by forfeit. Wanderers lost two games by forfeit.

Second Half Scores

Feb. 6, 1918   GWG
Montreal Canadiens 3 at Ottawa Senators 6   Dave Ritchie

Feb. 9, 1918
Toronto Hockey Club 7 at Montreal Canadiens 3   Ken Randall

Feb. 11, 1918
Ottawa Senators 1 at Toronto Hockey Club 3   Corb Denneny

Feb. 13, 1918
Toronto Hockey Club 6 at Ottawa Senators 1   Reg Noble

Feb. 16, 1918
Ottawa Senators 4 at Montreal Canadiens 10   Jack McDonald

Feb. 18, 1918
Montreal Canadiens 9 at Toronto Hockey Club 0   Didier Pitre

Feb. 20, 1918
Toronto Hockey Club 4 at Montreal Canadiens 5 (OT)   Jack McDonald

Feb. 23, 1918
Ottawa Senators 3 at Toronto Arenas 9   Harry Meeking

Feb. 25, 1918
Montreal Canadiens 0 at Ottawa Senators 8   Georges Boucher

Feb. 27, 1918
Ottawa Senators 3 Montreal Canadiens 1   Frank Nighbor
(Game played in Quebec City)

March 2, 1918
Montreal Canadiens 3 at Toronto Hockey Club 5   Ken Randall

March 6, 1918
Toronto Hockey Club 3 at Ottawa Senators 9   Frank Nighbor

TEAM	GP	W	L	F	A	P	H	A	OT
Toronto Hockey Club-x	8	5	3	37	34	10	3–1	2–2	0–1
Montreal Canadiens	8	3	5	34	37	6	2–1	1–3	1–0
Ottawa Senators-y	8	4	4	35	35	8	3–1	0–3	0–0

X- Winning second half title put Toronto into NHL playoffs
Y- Senators and Canadiens played one neutral site game in Quebec City, won by Ottawa

Three or More Goal Games

Player/Team	Date	Goals	Opponent (Goalie)
Cy Denneny, Ottawa Senators	Dec. 19, 1917	3	Mtl. Cdns. (Georges Vezina)
Harry Hyland, Mtl. Wanderers	Dec. 19, 1917	5	Toronto (Sammy Hebert 3; Arthur Brooks 2)
Reg Noble, Toronto	Dec. 19, 1917	4	Mtl. Wanderers (Bert Lindsay)
Joe Malone, Mtl. Cdns.	Dec. 19, 1917	5	Ottawa (Clint Benedict)
Newsy Lalonde, Mtl. Cdns.	Dec. 22, 1917	3	Mtl. Wanderers (Bert Lindsay)
Joe Malone, Mtl. Cdns. (2)	Dec. 22, 1917	3	Mtl. Wanderers (Bert Lindsay)
Cy Denneny, Ottawa Senators (2)	Dec. 22, 1917	3	Toronto (Arthur Brooks)
Corb Denneny, Toronto	Dec. 22, 1917	3	Ottawa (Clint Benedict)
Reg Noble, Toronto(2)	Dec. 22, 1917	4	Ottawa (Clint Benedict)
Bert Corbeau, Mtl. Cdns.	Dec. 26, 1917	3	Toronto (Arthur Brooks)
Harry Cameron, Toronto	Dec. 26, 1917	4	Mtl. Cdns. (Georges Vezina)
Cy Denneny, Ottawa Senators (3)	Dec. 29, 1917	4	Mtl. Wanderers (Bert Lindsay)

Appendix 1

Newsy Lalonde, Mtl. Cdns. (2)	Dec. 29, 1917	4	Toronto (Arthur Brooks)
Eddie Gerard, Ottawa	Jan. 2, 1918	3	Toronto (Sammy Hebert)
Newsy Lalonde, Mtl. Cdns. (3)	Jan. 5, 1918	3	Ottawa (Clint Benedict)
Joe Malone, Mtl. Cdns. (3)	Jan. 12, 1918	5	Ottawa (Clint Benedict)
Jack Darragh, Ottawa Senators	Jan. 14, 1918	3	Toronto (Harry (Hap) Holmes)
Cy Denneny, Ottawa (4)	Jan. 14, 1918	3	Toronto (Harry (Hap) Holmes)
Corb Denneny, Toronto (2)	Jan. 14, 1918	3	Ottawa (Clint Benedict)
Didier Pitre, Mtl. Cdns.	Jan. 19, 1918	3	Toronto (Harry (Hap) Holmes)
Joe Hall, Mtl. Cdns.	Jan. 21, 1918	3	Ottawa (Clint Benedict)
Harry Hyland, Ottawa Senators (2)	Jan. 23, 1918	3	Mtl. Cdns. (Georges Vezina)
Joe Malone, Mtl. Cdns. (4)	Jan. 30, 1918	4	Ottawa (Clint Benedict)
Joe Malone, Mtl. Cdns. (5)	Feb. 2, 1918	5	Toronto (Harry (Hap) Holmes)
Didier Pitre, Mtl. Cdns. (2)	Feb. 2, 1918	3	Toronto (Harry (Hap) Holmes)
Reg Noble, Toronto (3)	Feb. 4, 1918	3	Ottawa (Clint Benedict)
Cy Denneny, Ottawa Senators (5)	Feb. 6, 1918	3	Mtl. Cdns. (Georges Vezina)
Jack McDonald, Mtl. Cdns.	Feb. 16, 1918	3	Ottawa (Clint Benedict)
Joe Malone, Mtl. Cdns. (6)	Feb. 16, 1918	4	Ottawa (Clint Benedict)
Joe Malone, Mtl. Cdns. (7)	Feb. 20, 1918	3	Toronto (Harry (Hap) Holmes)
Reg Noble, Toronto (4)	Feb. 20, 1918	3	Mtl. Cdns. (Georges Vezina)
Reg Noble, Toronto (5)	Feb. 23, 1918	3	Ottawa (Clint Benedict)
Cy Denneny, Ottawa (6)	Feb. 25, 1918	3	Mtl. Cdns. (Georges Vezina)
Harry Cameron, Toronto (2)	March 2, 1918	3	Mtl. Cdns. (Georges Vezina)
Frank Nighbor, Ottawa	March 6, 1918	4	Toronto (Harry (Hap) Holmes)
Cy Denneny, Ottawa (7)	March 6, 1918	3	Toronto (Harry (Hap) Holmes)

(Career totals in brackets)

Shutouts

Goaltender/Team	Date	Result
Georges Vezina, Mtl. Cdns.	Feb. 18, 1918	Mtl. Cdns. 9 at Toronto 0
Clint Benedict, Ottawa	Feb. 25, 1918	Mtl. Cdns. 0 at Ottawa 8

NHL Playoffs

March 11, 1918   GWG
Montreal Canadiens 3 at Toronto Hockey Club 7   Harry Meeking

March 13, 1918
Toronto Hockey Club 3 at Montreal Canadiens 4   Newsy Lalonde
(Toronto wins two game, total goals series 10–7)

Three or More Goal Games

Player/Team	Date	Goals	Opponent (Goalie)
Harry Meeking, Toronto	March 11, 1918	3	Mtl. Cdns. (Georges Vezina)

Stanley Cup

Toronto (NHL) vs. Vancouver (PCHA)
March 20, 1918   GWG
Vancouver Millionaires 3 at Toronto Hockey Club 5   Alf Skinner

March 23, 1918
Vancouver Millionaires 6 at Toronto Hockey Club 4   Si Griffis

March 26, 1918
Vancouver Millionaires 3 at Toronto Hockey Club 6   Harry Cameron

March 28, 1918
Vancouver Millionaires 8 at Toronto Hockey Club 1   Barney Stanley

March 30, 1918
Vancouver Millionaires 1 at Toronto Hockey Club 2   Corb Denneny
(Toronto wins best-of-five series three games to two).
Note: Games 1, 3 and 5 played by NHL rules; Games 2 and 4 played
by PCHA rules.

Three or More Goal Games

Player/Team	Date	Goals	Opponent (Goalie)
Duncan MacKay, Vancouver	March 23, 1918	3	Toronto (Harry Holmes)
Alf Skinner, Toronto	March 23, 1918	3	Vancouver (Hugh Lehman)

APPENDIX 2

NHL Firsts

First Goal: Dave Ritchie, Montreal Wanderers

First Assist: Dave Ritchie, Montreal Wanderers

First Penalty: Art Ross, Montreal Wanderers

First Win: Bert Lindsay, Montreal Wanderers

First Shutout: Georges Vezina, Montreal Canadiens

First Hat Trick: Harry Hyland, Montreal Wanderers

First Major Penalty: Ken Randall, Toronto Hockey Club

First Match Penalties: Didier Pitre, Montreal Canadiens; Ken Randall, Toronto Hockey Club

First Fighting Majors: Didier Pitre, Montreal Canadiens; Ken Randall, Toronto Hockey Club

Trophy Case

There were no individual awards presented during the NHL's inaugural season of 1917–18. But what if the major awards presented today were up for grabs back then? Who would the winners have been?

Hart Trophy (MVP)

Winner: Joe Malone, Montreal Canadiens

A scoring machine, Malone potted 44 goals in 20 games for a per-game average of 2.2 that remains an NHL single-season record. His 44-goal total stood as the NHL standard until Rocket Richard scored 50 for the Habs in 1943–44.

Runner-up: Harry (Hap) Holmes, Toronto Hockey Club

There was no doubt Toronto's lineup was worthy of competing for an NHL title. All the team lacked was an NHL-calibre goaltender. When the rights to Holmes were acquired from the defunct Montreal Wanderers, Toronto's goals against dropped from 6.6 per game to 4.73 and Toronto won the second-half title.

Art Ross Trophy
Winner: Joe Malone, Montreal Canadiens
Malone started fast, scoring five times in the season opener, one of three five-goal games he'd record. He finished with 44–4–48 totals. He'd also shared the scoring title in the last season of the NHA.

Runner-Up: Cy Denneny, Ottawa Senators
Denneny scored 36 goals but factoring in his 10 assists, he nearly usurped Malone's point total. The 10 helpers gave Denneny a share of the NHL lead in that category.

Norris Trophy
Winner: Harry Cameron, Toronto Hockey Club
Leading all defencemen with 17–10–27 numbers, Cameron finished sixth in NHL scoring, the highest a rearguard would place until Cameron was fourth in league scoring in 1921–22. His skill with the puck and speed on skates made Cameron a persistent threat.

Runner Up: Joe Hall, Montreal Canadiens
The veteran lived up to his nickname, as Bad Joe was the bad man of the league, leading the NHL with 100 penalty minutes. But Hall was a force at both ends of the ice, finishing with 8–7–15 totals.

Vezina Trophy
Winner: Georges Vezina, Montreal Canadiens
Fitting that the man for whom the trophy would be named would have won the trophy in the NHL's first campaign. Vezina posted the first shutout in league history and led the NHL with 12 wins and a 3.93 goals-against average.

Runner-Up: Harry (Hap) Holmes, Toronto Hockey Club
Holmes turned around the fortunes of the Toronto team when he was acquired seven games into the season. Only Vezina won more games and posted a lower GAA than Holmes (nine, 4.73).

Appendix 2

Lady Byng Trophy
Winner: Corb Denneny, Toronto Hockey Club
Potting 20 goals while collecting just 14 minutes in penalties, the lesser-known of the Denneny brothers played it clean in an era when vicious hockey was the norm.

Runner-Up: Frank Nighbor
Had he not missed the first half of the season while in the service of the Royal Flying Corps, Nighbor would have won this award going away. He scored 11 goals and 19 points in 10 games while serving just two minor penalties. Nighbor would win the first two Lady Byngs in 1924–25 and 1925–26.

Calder Trophy
Winner: Jack Adams, Toronto Hockey Club
In a season where only four rookies played, Adams was the best of a thin bunch. Though he didn't collect a point, Adams took a regular turn almost from the moment Toronto signed him in February.

Runner-Up: Morley Bruce, Ottawa Senators
Bruce was seeing plenty of ice time as a first-year defenceman with the Sens and had he not been called up for military service at mid-season, this award would have likely been his.

NHL All-Stars

First Team	Position	Second Team
Georges Vezina, Canadiens	Goal	Hap Holmes, Toronto
Harry Cameron, Toronto	Defence	Buck Boucher, Ottawa
Joe Hall, Canadiens	Defence	Bert Corbeau, Canadiens
Newsy Lalonde, Canadiens	Centre	Corb Denneny, Toronto
Joe Malone, Canadiens	Left Wing	Cy Denneny, Ottawa
Didier Pitre, Canadiens	Right Wing	Jack Darragh, Ottawa

ACKNOWLEDGEMENTS

The author wishes to thank Dan Wells, Chris Andrechek and all the staff at Biblioasis for their non-stop effort in making this project a reality. A Jaromir Jagr salute is also offered to Art Ross, Newsy Lalonde, Georges Vezina, Clint Benedict and all of the pioneers who played during that first NHL season. Most of all, let's not forget the fans of the game, without whom the NHL would have never grown from its infancy into the century-old major league entity that it is today.

ABOUT THE AUTHOR

Bob Duff has covered the NHL since 1988 and is a contributor to *The Hockey News, HockeyBuzz.com, NHL.com*, and *TAP Digital Marketing*. Duff's book credits include *Marcel Pronovost: A Life in Hockey, The China Wall: The Timeless Legend of Johnny Bower, Original Six Dynasties: Detroit Red Wings, Without Fear, Nine: Salute to Mr. Hockey, On the Wing: A History of the Windsor Spitfires*, and *The Hockey Hall of Fame MVP Trophies and Winners*.